Jesus
Reconsidered

Best wishes, Dick!

Perry Lea

Jesus
Seminar
Guides

Bernard Brandon Scott, series editor

Published volumes

Volume 1: Jesus Reconsidered: Scholarship in the Public Eye

Volume 2: Listening to the Parables of Jesus

Jesus
Reconsidered

Scholarship in
the Public Eye

Bernard Brandon Scott, editor

POLEBRIDGE PRESS
Santa Rosa, California

Cover and interior design by Robaire Ream

Library of Congress Cataloging-in-Publication Data
Jesus reconsidered : scholarship in the public eye / [edited by] Bernard
Brandon Scott .
        p. cm. -- (Jesus seminar guides)
    Includes bibliographical references.
    ISBN 978-1-59815-002-5
    1. Jesus Christ--Historicity. 2. Jesus Christ--History of doctrines. 3.
Jesus Seminar. I. Scott, Bernard Brandon, 1941-
    BT303.2.J468 2007
    232.9'08--dc22
                                            2007032131

Table of Contents

Series Preface

Westar Institute, the home of the Jesus Seminar, is an advocate for literacy in religion and the Bible. A member-supported, non-profit research and educational institute, its mission is to foster collaborative research in religious studies and to communicate the results of the scholarship of religion to a broad, non-specialist public. Through publications, educational programs, and research projects like the Jesus Seminar, Westar brings Fellows of the Institute—scholars with advanced degrees in biblical studies, religion, or related fields—into conversation with non-specialists from all walks of life.

Westar's series, *Jesus Seminar Guides*, is designed to gather the best writings of Westar Fellows from the pages of its membership magazine, *The Fourth R*, its academic journal, *Forum*, and occasionally from previously unpublished material. Arranged topically, the *Guides* summarize the important questions and debates that have driven the work of the Jesus Seminar over the last twenty years. They are intended for use in classrooms, discussion groups inside and outside churches, and for the general reader.

Contributors

Marcus J. Borg is Hundere Distinguished Professor of Religion and Culture at Oregon State University. He has written eleven books, including *Meeting Jesus Again for the First Time* (1994) the best-selling book by a contemporary Jesus scholar; *The God We Never Knew*, named as one of "ten best books" in religion for 1997; and *Reading the Bible Again for the First Time* (2001), another bestseller. He has served as national chair of the Historical Jesus Section of the Society of Biblical Literature, co-chair of its International New Testament Program Committee, and president of the Anglican Association of Biblical Scholars.

Robert W. Funk was the founder of the Jesus Seminar and of the Westar Institute. A Guggenheim Fellow and Senior Fulbright Scholar, he served as Annual Professor of the American School of Oriental Research in Jerusalem and as chair of the Graduate Department of Religion at Vanderbilt University. He was a recognized pioneer in modern biblical scholarship, having led the Society of Biblical Literature as its Executive Secretary from 1968–1973. His many books include *The Five Gospels* (1993) and *The Acts of Jesus* (1998) (both with the Jesus Seminar) and *Honest to Jesus* (1996), *A Credible Jesus* (2002), and *Funk on Parables* (2006).

Roy W. Hoover is Weyerhaeuser Professor of Biblical Literature and Professor of Religion Emeritus, Whitman College. A Fellow of the Jesus Seminar since 1986, he wrote a number of the papers that served as the basis for the Seminar's deliberations and has been a frequent participant in the Jesus Seminar on the Road Program. Roy Hoover is co-author (with Robert W. Funk) of *The Five Gospels* (1993), and editor of *Profiles of Jesus* (2002). His published articles have appeared in *Harvard Theological Review, Forum, The Fourth R,* and *Bible*

Review. In 1992, he received the Whitman College Award for Faculty Achievement.

Perry V. Kea is Associate Professor of Biblical Studies and the chairperson of the Philosophy and Religion Department at the University of Indianapolis. He is co-editor of *Perspectives on New Testament Ethics* (with Andrew K. M. Adam) and has contributed several papers to the deliberations of the Jesus Seminar.

Robert J. Miller is Associate Professor of Religious Studies at Juniata College in Pennsylvania. He is the editor of *The Complete Gospels* (1992), an anthology of twenty early gospels presented in Westar's innovative translation, the Scholars Version, and author of *The Jesus Seminar and Its Critics* (1999) and *Born Divine* (2003). In 1996, he was awarded the Midway College Trustee Award for Faculty Excellence.

Ruth Schweitzer-Mordecdai is a minister of the United Church of Christ and a Marriage, Family and Child Counselor practicing in Marin County, California. An associate member of the Westar Institute, she is the author of *Spiritual Freedom: Healing Shame-Based Spirituality* (1993).

Bernard Brandon Scott is the Darbeth Distinguished Professor of New Testament at the Phillips Theological Seminary, Tulsa, Oklahoma. He is the author of several books, including *Hear Then the Parable* (1989), *Re-Imagine the World* (2002) and *Hollywood Dreams and Biblical Stories* (co-edited with Robert Funk and James R. Butts, 1994), *The Parables of Jesus: Red Letter Edition* (1988) the first report of the Jesus Seminar, *Reading New Testament Greek* (co-authored with a group of students, 1993), and the editor of Robert W. Funk, *Funk on Parables* (2006).

Introduction

Bernard Brandon Scott

The Jesus Seminar consists of scholars who come together to study issues related to Jesus, his first-century environment and the growth of early Christianity. Often referred to by the press and by critics alike as a single voice, it is not, in fact, monolithic. Scholars are notoriously independent and contrary. The scholars of the Jesus Seminar are no different. They represent a multitude of perspectives and a wide range of opinion. The oft-heard statement, "the Jesus Seminar says," is hardly an accurate depiction.

The "voice" of the Seminar is its publications, especially *The Five Gospels* and *The Acts of Jesus*. They report a consensus based on votes taken following intense discussion and, at times, fierce debate. The votes reflect a minority as well as a majority opinion. Fellows of the Jesus Seminar have been heard to describe the Seminar experience as akin to an intense post-doctoral seminar. Over the years, the Fellows have developed a sense of community and a degree of collegiality that defines the Seminar and distinguishes it from the usual academic discourse.

1

The Seminar has been dogged by controversy and notoriety.
While most scholars do not work in an ivory tower, they do
live quiet lives. So, for many, the notoriety was hard to understand (even though the Seminar's founder, Robert W. Funk,
clearly anticipated it from the beginning). After all, we were
only making public what had been well known within the
walls of the academy for more than a hundred years. But that,
it turns out, was the very cause of the controversy—we made
public what had been hidden, and we forced into the open
a discussion that had previously been held in private. Had it
been otherwise, we would not have encountered an audience
so woefully uninformed on religious matters.

The Seminar set out to accomplish a project that had never
been attempted before: (1) to summarize what modern scholarship knew about the historical Jesus and (2) to make its findings available to the general public. As you read these essays be
sure to keep both of these goals in mind. They define the task
the Seminar members set out to solve.

The Seminar began its work in two phases. The first, beginning in 1985 and running until Spring 1991, concerned the
words of Jesus. What did he actually say? *The Five Gospels*
(1993) presented this material to the public. The second stage
ran from Fall 1991 until Fall 1995 and resulted in *The Acts of
Jesus* (1998). The following essays offer a more than adequate
description of the Seminar's history and procedures.

Funk was the originator and impresario of the Jesus
Seminar. His inaugural address to those forty plus scholars who
came together for the first Jesus Seminar in Berkeley, CA, in
March 1985, leads this collection. It did not originally appear
in *The Fourth R*, but *Forum*, the scholarly journal of Westar, so
it is appropriate to make it available here for a more general
audience. Funk anticipated the controversy that would result
from going public with the results of scholarship. While not all
his ambitious goals have been achieved, it is remarkable how
his outline for a new form of public, collaborative scholarship has come to pass. Scholarship in public has been one of
the Seminar's singular achievements. In 1985 Funk already
anticipated the danger in a religiously illiterate public. "The
religious establishment has not allowed the intelligence of high

scholarship to pass through pastors and priests to a hungry laity, and the radio and TV counterparts of educated clergy have traded in platitudes and pieties and played on the igno-rance of the uninformed. A rude and rancorous awakening lies ahead."

Both Roy Hoover and Marcus Borg provide early assess-ments of the Seminar as a work in progress. It is interesting to note, in particular, their various readings of the meaning of the gray votes.

My essay, evaluating the Seminar after it had finished its work, was published following Robert Funk's death. It assesses the gains of the Seminar and lays out a path for the future.

Perry Kea's contribution demonstrates that the Jesus Seminar belongs to a long tradition of scholarship, that it did not invent the quest for the historical Jesus *ex nihilo*, out of nothing. He outlines the ebb and flow of the quest and the various questions that have driven it.

The last three essays turn to the controversy generated by the Seminar's findings. Ruth Schweitzer-Mordecai, a minis-ter of the UCC church and an associate member of Westar, employs the methods of the family systems theory and con-cludes that the criticism of the Seminar indicates that often we are involved in dysfunctional "families," collectively called the church. She accurately describes the shock of many semi-nary students when they first confront the findings of histori-cal scholarship about the Bible and notes their anger at this discovery.

Roy Hoover responds to a critique of the Jesus Seminar by a group of evangelical scholars, published in *Jesus under Fire*, by pointing out that their principles do not allow them to do actual history. Ironically, given their position, the histori-cal Jesus does not count. In an interview Robert Miller also discusses critics and criticisms of the Seminar. Miller's work in this regard eventually led to his own book, *The Jesus Seminar and Its Critics.*

These essays gather together efforts of members of the Jesus Seminar to explain what they are about and to defend that effort. As such, they are not only an introduction to the work of the Seminar, but the beginnings of its history.

Chapter One

The Issue of Jesus

Robert W. Funk

The opening remarks of Jesus Seminar
Chairman Funk, presented at the first
meeting held March 21-24, 1985,
in Berkeley, California

We are about to embark on a momentous enterprise. We are going to inquire simply, rigorously after the voice of Jesus, after what he really said.

In this process, we will be asking a question that borders the sacred, that even abuts blasphemy, for many in our society. As a consequence, the course we shall follow may prove hazardous. We may well provoke hostility. But we will set out, in spite of the dangers, because we are professionals and because the issue of Jesus is there to be faced, much as Mt. Everest confronts the team of climbers.

We are not embarking on this venture in a corner. We are going to carry out our work in full public view; we will not only honor the freedom of information, we will insist on the public disclosure of our work and, insofar as it lies within our power, we shall see to it that the public is informed of our judgments. We shall do so not because our wisdom is superior, but because we are committed to public accountability.

Forum 1,1 (March 1985), pp. 7–12

Our basic plan is simple. We intend to examine every frag-
ment of the traditions attached to the name of Jesus in order
to determine what he really said—not his literal words, perhaps, but the substance and style of his utterances. We are in
quest of his *voice,* insofar as it can be distinguished from many
other voices also preserved in the tradition. We are prepared
to bring to bear everything we know and can learn about the
form and content, about the formation and transmission, of
aphorisms and parables, dialogues and debates, attributed or
attributable to Jesus, in order to carry out our task.

There are profound and more obvious reasons we have
decided to undertake this work. The more profound and complex reasons may be deferred until a subsequent session of
the Seminar. A statement of the more patent motivations will
serve this occasion adequately.

We are launching these collective investigations in the first
instance in response to our students, past, present, and future.
Once our students learn to discern the traditions of the New
Testament and other early Christian literature—and they all do
to a greater or lesser extent under our tutelage—they want to
know the ultimate truth: what did Jesus really say? Who was this
man to whom the tradition steadily refers itself? For a change,
we will be answering a question that is really being asked.

Make no mistake: there is widespread and passionate interest
in this issue, even among those uninitiated in the higher mys-
teries of gospel scholarship. The religious establishment has not
allowed the intelligence of high scholarship to pass through
pastors and priests to a hungry laity, and the radio and TV
counterparts of educated clergy have traded in platitudes and
pieties and played on the ignorance of the uninformed. A rude
and rancorous awakening lies ahead.

What we are about takes courage, as I said. We are probing
what is most sacred to millions, and hence we will constantly
border on blasphemy. We must be prepared to forebear the
hostility we shall provoke. At the same time, our work, if carefully and thoughtfully wrought, will spell liberty for other
millions. It is for the latter that we labor.

We are forming this Seminar in the second place because
we are entering an exciting new period of biblical, especially
New Testament, scholarship.

We have new and tantalizing primary sources with which to work, such as the *Gospel of Thomas,* the *Apocryphon of James,* the *Dialogue of the Savior,* and we stand on the verge of new study instruments, such as the *New Gospel Parallels,* the new *Sayings Parallels,* and perhaps even a new and more tolerable translation of other New Testament apocrypha.

Beyond these advances, we have learned to transcend the paradigms of scholarship set for us early in this century. We have learned our textual criticism, our source and form and redaction criticism, we have taken in the best—and some of the worst—of our German and English and French predecessors. But we are now moving on to different paradigms: to parables and aphorisms as metaphors and poetry, to narratology, to reader-response criticism, to social description and analysis, and to many other promising ventures. We are laying new foundations in editing and publishing primary source materials, new and old, and are building new edifices of interpretation on those foundations.

Perhaps most important of all, these developments have taken place predominantly, though not exclusively, in American scholarship. We need not promote chauvinism; we need only recognize that American biblical scholarship threatens to come of age, and that in itself is a startling new stage in our academic history. We may even be approaching the time when Europeans, if they know what they are about, will come to North America on sabbaticals to catch up, rather than the other way around. It is already clear that Europeans who do not read American scholarship are falling steadily behind.

The acknowledgment that a bonafide tradition of American New Testament scholarship is aborning brings me to the second large point of these introductory remarks. Creating a tradition of scholarship means that our work must finally and firmly become cumulative.

Cumulative is defined in law as evidence that gives greater weight to evidence previously introduced. In banking, cumulative interest is interest on both principal and accumulated interest. Scholarship is cumulative that lays down successive layers of evidence and interpretation of preceding layers.

I invite you to ponder the more than sixty books written by Fellows of this Seminar and its patron saints (Amos N.

Wilder, Norman Perrin, Fred O. Francis). In some important respects these books represent cumulative effort: in and
through these works a new tradition of scholarship is being
formed. But in many respects, our work remains fragmented
and isolated. We too often set about reinventing the wheel for
each new vehicle we attempt to design and build. We are too
often ignorant of each other's achievements. As a consequence,
we tend to repeat the same major projects. Yet this phase of
our history is coming to an end, as the emergence of this
Seminar will attest.

In order to abet cumulative scholarship, I want to propose two preliminary steps. First, I am requesting Fellows of
the Seminar to prepare prose accounts of their careers to be
published in *Forum*. These autobiographical sketches should
indicate something of one's intellectual odyssey as well as the
principal stations of endeavor along the way. In other words,
we need to know the movements and pauses of our colleagues,
in order better to understand how we got where we are. And
it would make these sketches more interesting reading were
they to include hints of the human.

As a second step, I am requesting that each Fellow provide
a comprehensive bibliography of his or her publications for
Forum. With the appearance of these bibliographies, Fellows
need no longer be ignorant of the work of colleagues.

Beyond these two items, I am further suggesting that we
review, in some depth, works of Fellows that are relevant for
the Seminar. We have begun with Crossan's *In Fragments* and
Four Other Gospels. These reviews will be published in *Forum*,
of course. We should proceed to other works. I am subsequently going to propose that we tackle M. Eugene Boring's
Sayings of the Risen Jesus and the recent work of Werner Kelber.
But that will be only the beginning. I am herewith inviting
Fellows to submit reviews of any works published by other
Fellows for publication in *Forum*. If our work is to become
genuinely cumulative, we must become acquainted with
everything that has been produced.

These are only provisional steps that should lead up to the
work of the Seminar itself. In making an inventory of the Jesus
tradition and evaluating the items in that inventory, we must

lay the foundations carefully. And we must then build painstak-
ingly on those foundations. Only so will our work stand the
tests of consensus and time.

Our endeavors must be cumulative and reciprocal in the
last analysis in order to frame our individual proclivities and
eccentricities by the highest degree of scholarly objectivity. My
idiosyncrasies will be counterbalanced by your peculiarities.
Our common finitude will be baptized in collective wisdom.
(That does not make us gods, but it does obscure the con-
sequences of original sin.) The result will be a compromise:
not a sacrificing of integrity, but an acquiescence in the best
informed common judgment. Our end product may look like
a horse designed by a committee, that is, like a camel, but at
least it will be a beast of burden tough enough to withstand
the desert heat of powerful adverse criticism.

To heighten the risk of our program, I am proposing that
we conduct our work in full public view. If we are to survive
as scholars of the humanities, as well as theologians, we must
quit the academic closet. And we must begin to sell a product
that has some utilitarian value to someone—or which at least
appears to have utilitarian value to someone. We could begin
with our students—not a bad place to begin—but we could
also undertake to advise our president, who regards himself as
a Koine Kowboy [Ronald Reagan—ed.], about the perils of
apocalyptic foreign policy. And we might conceivably do so
on the basis of this Seminar, to the extent that he is willing,
not just to cite, but actually to heed, the words of Jesus. At all
events, we must begin earnestly to report on our work to a
wider public and then to engage that public in conversation
and conference.

I come now to the final point. It is a rather large one and
can be made here only in the skimpiest outline. It lies central
to all the other points I have made or will try to make in the
course of our investigations together.

Since we are Bible scholars, let us begin with the Bible as a
whole. The Bible begins, we are wont to say, at the Beginning
and concludes with a vision of the heavenly city, the ultimate
End. Traditionally, the Bible is taken as a coherent structure:
the Apocalypse is thought to bring things around again to

their original state; the evil introduced into the garden in the
first instance is eradicated in the last. And the beginning and
end are viewed as wholly consonant with the *real* events that
occur between them. Thus, the Christian savior figure is interpreted as belonging to the primeval innocence of the garden
and yet predicting and precipitating the final outcome.

There are two things to be said about this scheme. First, we
are having increasing difficulty these days in accepting the biblical account of the creation and of the apocalyptic conclusion
in anything like a literal sense. The difficulty just mentioned is
connected with a second feature: we now know that narrative
accounts of ourselves, our nation, the Western tradition, and
the history of the world, are fictions.

Narrative fictions, aside from recent experiments in "struc-
tureless" novels, must have a beginning and an end and be
located in space. They must involve a finite number of participants and obviously depict a limited number of events.
Moreover, it is required of narratives that there be some
fundamental continuity in participants and some connection
between and among events that form the narrative chain. It is
in this formal sense that the Bible is said to form a narrative
and to embrace in its several parts a coherent and continuous
structure. And it is also in this same sense that the Bible, along
with all our histories, is a fiction.

A fiction is thus a selection—arbitrary in nature—of
participants and events arranged in a connected chain and on
a chronological line with an arbitrary beginning and ending.
In sum, we make up all our "stories"—out of real enough
material, of course—in relation to imaginary constructs, within
temporal limits.

Our fictions, although deliberately fictive, are nevertheless
not subject to proof or falsification. We do not abandon them
because they are demonstrably false, but because they lose their
"operational effectiveness" (Kermode, 40), because they fail to
account for enough of what we take to be real in the everyday
course of events. Fictions of the sciences or of law are dis-
carded when they no longer match our living experience of
things. But religious fictions, like those found in the Bible, are
more tenacious because they "are harder to free from mythi-

cal 'deposit,'" as Frank Kermode puts it (Kermode, 40). "If we forget that fictions are fictive we regress to myth" (Kermode, 41). The Bible has become mostly myth in Kermode's sense of the term, since the majority in our society do not hold that the fictions of the Bible are indeed fictive.

Our dilemma is becoming acute: just as the beginning of the created world is receding in geological time before our very eyes, so the future no longer presents itself as naive imminence. Many of us believe that the world may be turned into cinder one day soon without an accompanying conviction that Armageddon is upon us. But our crisis goes beyond these terminal points: it affects the middle as well. Those of us who work with that hypothetical middle—Jesus of Nazareth—are hard pressed to concoct any form of coherence that will unite beginning, middle, and end in some grand new fiction that will meet all the requirements of narrative. To put the matter bluntly, we are having as much trouble with the middle—the messiah—as we are with the terminal points. What we need is a new fiction that takes as its starting point the central event in the Judeo-Christian drama and reconciles that middle with a new story that reaches beyond old beginnings and endings. In sum, we need a new narrative of Jesus, a new gospel, if you will, that places Jesus differently in the grand scheme, the epic story.

Not any fiction will do. The fiction of the superiority of the Aryan race led to the extermination of six million Jews. The fiction of American superiority prompted the massacre of thousands of Native Americans and the Vietnam War. The fiction of Revelation keeps many common folk in bondage to ignorance and fear. We require a new, liberating fiction, one that squares with the best knowledge we can now accumulate and one that transcends self-serving ideologies. And we need a fiction that we recognize to be fictive.

Satisfactions will come hard. Anti-historicist criticism, now rampant among us, will impugn every fact we seek to establish. Every positive attribution will be challenged again and again. All of this owes, of course, to what Oscar Wilde called "the decay of lying"; we have fallen, he says, into "careless habits of accuracy" (quoted by Kermode, 43). And yet, as Kermode reminds us, "the survival of the paradigms is as much our business as their erosion" (Kermode, 43). Our stories are eroding under the acids of historical criticism. We must retell our stories. And there is one epic story that has Jesus in it.

Chapter Two

The Work of the Jesus Seminar

Honesty Collaboration Accessibility

A Defense of the Seminar and a Response to Its Critics

Roy W. Hoover

Introduction

The Jesus Seminar has been generating news stories ever since it was founded almost twelve years ago. *Time* magazine observed last year that "it would be hard to find a newspaper in America that hasn't done a story on the Jesus Seminar over the past decade." Inevitably newspaper stories have reported the work of the Seminar in piecemeal fashion, since they often published the results of one of the Seminar's semi-annual meetings. Often such stories have focused on the controversy the Seminar was provoking and included responses to the Seminar's work by outsiders, many of whom viewed the Seminar through thick filters of entrenched opinion or traditional belief. In many instances the outsiders' views were given equal space, sometimes more than equal space.

My aim is to tell a more connected story of the Seminar's work as seen from the inside. I will do this in three parts: (1) how the Seminar came into being and why; (2) how the Seminar does its work; and (3) what the Seminar has accom-

The Fourth R 9,5–6 (September/December 1996), pp. 9–15

plished so far and aims to do next. In the course of doing this
I will respond to several criticisms of the Seminar's work.

How the Seminar Came
Into Being and Why

The Jesus Seminar began in 1985 when Robert Funk invited
thirty scholars to join him in reopening the question of the
historical Jesus. In March of that year twenty-one of the thirty
met at the Graduate Theological Union in Berkeley to begin
the work that has continued now for over a decade. At that
first session Robert Funk offered some opening remarks. This
is how he began:

> We are about to embark on a momentous enterprise. We
> are going to inquire simply, rigorously after the *voice* of
> Jesus, after what he really said. In this process, we will be
> asking a question that borders the sacred, that even abuts
> blasphemy, for many in our society. As a consequence,
> the course we shall follow may prove hazardous. We may
> well provoke hostility. But we will set out, in spite of the
> dangers, because we are professionals and because the
> issue of Jesus is there to be faced, much as Mt. Everest
> confronts the team of climbers.
>
> We are not embarking on this venture in a corner.
> We are going to carry out our work in full public
> view . . . and, in so far as it lies within our power, we shall
> see to it that the public is informed of our judgments.
> We shall do so, not because our wisdom is superior, but
> because we are committed to public accountability.
>
> Our basic plan is simple. We intend to examine every
> [piece of ancient tradition] attached to the name of Jesus
> in order to determine what he really said—not his literal
> words, perhaps, but the substance and style of his utter-
> ances. We are in quest of his voice, insofar as it can be
> distinguished from many other voices also preserved in
> the tradition. We are prepared to bring to bear everything
> we know and can learn about the form and content,
> about the formation and transmission of aphorisms and
> parables, dialogues and debates, attributed to or attribut-
> able to Jesus, in order to carry out our task.

Those remarks of the founder of the Seminar, which subsequently appeared in the journal *Forum,* are the first published statements about its aims.

What led up to the founding of the Seminar was the recognition by Funk and his colleagues that scholarship on the gospels had entered a new era and called for new initiatives. New primary sources had become available, most notably the Dead Sea scrolls (1947) and the Nag Hammadi codices (1945), and new paradigms of scholarship had been created. Together they opened up new possibilities for historical interpretation. Two of these developments in scholarship were especially important in creating the bases upon which the Seminar began its work.

One is what some have characterized as the rediscovery of the parables of Jesus. In the late 1960s and the 1970s the Parables Seminar of the Society of Biblical Literature, the oldest and largest professional society in North America for biblical scholars, broke new ground in research on parables. Among the participants in the Parables Seminar were a number of scholars who subsequently became Fellows of the Jesus Seminar, including John Dominic Crossan, Bernard Brandon Scott, Lane McGaughy, and Jesus Seminar founder Robert Funk. Other well-known scholars also participated, including Norman Perrin, Dan Via, and Amos Wilder. In *Honest to Jesus,* Robert Funk writes that the work of the Parables Seminar resulted in a new view of the parables of Jesus "as literary and aesthetic entities in their own right, with their own integrity and with new interpretive potential." For the members of the Parables Seminar, "that discovery changed everything" (68). They now saw the parables as conveying meanings that differed from those of Jesus the apocalyptic prophet whose profile had dominated historical Jesus scholarship since Albert Schweitzer published his classic book *The Quest of the Historical Jesus* in 1906.

The second development in scholarship that has informed the work of the Seminar from its beginning was the rediscovery of the wisdom tradition in the Hebrew Bible and in Judaism, together with the recognition of the sapiential character of many of the sayings of Jesus transmitted in the gospel tradition. Analytical studies of the Synoptic Sayings Source (Q) by scholars Helmut Koester and James Robinson and more

recently extended by John Kloppenborg, Burton Mack, and
other scholars participating in the International Q Project
produced a substantial case for the view that the earliest layer
in the stratigraphy of Q consisted of wisdom sayings and that
the eschatological sayings in the Q collection appear to have
been later additions.

Further, the demonstration by Helmut Koester (pp. 84–124)
and Crossan that the sayings tradition transmitted in the
Gospel of Thomas is not dependent on the canonical gospels,
but represents independent tradition, sometimes in forms that
are more original than their parallels in versions of Q that
appear in Matthew and Luke, and the recognition of wisdom as the theme of Thomas added support to the idea that
the historical Jesus might appropriately be characterized as a
teacher of wisdom of an iconoclastic sort.

So the primary reason for the founding of the Jesus Seminar
was the arrival of a new and promising moment in the history
of New Testament scholarship, a convergence of new historical
sources and new ways to build on the achievements of earlier
scholarship. And the first aim of the Seminar was to use and
extend the new scholarship to expand the horizon of what we
can know about Jesus as a figure of history and about the origin of our religious heritage.

But the Jesus Seminar has had a second aim from its beginning as well, and that is to make the fruits of biblical scholarship available and accessible to the general public. Despite the
valiant efforts of some scholars, the results of modern biblical
scholarship are little known by the public, or even by people
who attend church regularly. The gulf between biblical education in the seminaries and biblical knowledge in the pews
continues to be widely acknowledged. The decision of the
Jesus Seminar to go public with the results of its work was
motivated by the judgment that important results of biblical scholarship ought to be visible to and discussable by any
church-goer or any member of the general public who might
be interested to learn about such matters; and by the judgment
that if understandings of religion alternative to those dissemi-
nated by television evangelists were to become more widely
known, the general welfare of society would be well served.

If our scholarship is worth doing, then its worth ought to be communicated to the public and not only to other scholars. For such reasons as these, the Jesus Seminar has been going public on purpose from the beginning.

The Jesus Seminar has met twice each year from the beginning. Members volunteer, or are asked, to write critical papers on the announced agenda in advance of the meeting. Copies of the papers are mailed about a month before the meeting to Fellows who plan to attend. At the meeting we focus on the issues that are posed by the texts on which the papers have been written. We discuss, question, nit-pick, argue, defend our views or change our minds. Then we vote, by marking a ballot or by choosing one of those now famous colored beads and dropping it into a small box.

Some scholars have regarded our practice of voting as inappropriate or even ludicrous, making it look as if questions about historicity could be determined by a majority vote—a notion possible only in America, it is said. The criticism is as foolish as the parody invented for it. Such voting does not establish the truth of a matter, nor does it decide the historicity of a piece of evidence; but voting does record a judgment. It is an exercise in intellectual honesty when a scholar declares his or her best judgment about important and complicated matters rather than taking shelter behind the shield of learned equivocations. Or as Dom Crossan said about the publication of the Seminar's red letter edition of *The Parables of Jesus,* it is "a red letter day for the ethics of scholarship, for the moral demand that thinkers state clearly, openly, and honestly what are their sources, their methods, and their results, and, above all, that they come before the eschaton to conclusion and consensus." Furthermore, voting on matters related to the biblical text has some distinguished precedents. Committees of scholars who have produced a critical edition of the Greek New Testament have voted on which of the variant readings in the manuscripts is most likely the more original; and Bible translation committees have voted on which of several possible renderings of a term or a phrase should be adopted for their version. And in the next edition both committees have been known to change their minds.

Ecumenical councils take votes also. On April 8, 1546, for
example, the Council of Trent adopted Jerome's Vulgate edition
as sacred and canonical by a vote of twenty-four to fifteen,
with sixteen abstentions. So the Council settled the question of the canon by a minority vote: only forty-four percent
of those present and eligible voted in the affirmative.[1] If this
result were converted to the Jesus Seminar's method of assign-
ing a color according to a weighted average, and if we assumed
that the twenty-four yeas were a fifty/fifty mix of red and pink
votes, that the fifteen nays were black votes, and that the sixteen abstentions were gray votes, that would yield a weighted
average of .46, a gray vote!

Much has been made of the fact that the Seminar found
sufficient evidence of historicity for only about eighteen percent of the sayings attributed to Jesus in the ancient sources
to color them red or pink in *The Five Gospels*. The most common reaction to that finding is surprise or shock, in some cases
even outrage, at such a small percentage of historically authentic sayings. But I would suggest that this result shows that the
Seminar took the question of the burden of proof seriously:
the burden of proof belongs to the one who makes a claim for
the historicity of a saying. The claim of historicity is only as
good as the case one can make for it. Some of our critics have
declined to accept the burden of proof in making their claims.
They seem to be more concerned with defending the theological authority of the text than with assessing the historicity
of the sayings attributed to Jesus in the text.

What has received too little attention is the significance of
the gray and black votes. Sayings voted black are thus identi-
fied as the voice of a gospel author or of the early church
rather than the voice of Jesus. The first thing one gains from
this assessment is clarity. Surely clarity is always preferable to
confusion or to being misled, isn't it? The second thing to
be gained from the black vote is an appreciation of the other
voices heard in these texts. No doubt they spoke because of
what Jesus had spoken, because of what Jesus had done, and

---

1. Metzger, *The Canon of the New Testament*, reports and comments
on the vote at the Council of Trent, p. 246.

because such words and deeds had cost him his life. But they also have some significant things to say on their own. The black vote invites us to recognize and appreciate their views. Noticing the freedom they exercised in expressing their views might move us to exercise the liberty and find the courage to voice things significant for our own time.

The gray vote merits attention also. Gray is the color of doubt, but the doubt can be of more than one kind. Sometimes when I voted gray the doubt corresponded to the way the Seminar defined the color early on: "Jesus did not say this, but the ideas contained in it are close to his own." Sometimes when I voted gray I meant, "I don't think Jesus said this, but I'm not entirely sure." Sometimes the resulting gray vote was simply statistical evidence that there was no consensus among the Fellows of the Seminar at all. The votes were spread across the whole spectrum from red to black. One might say, then, that the gray vote is both a caution and an invitation: a caution against smoothing things over, or resolving the burden of proof question too conveniently, and an invitation to revisit a datum voted gray, if one can show there is sufficient warrant. In short, there is more significance in each of the colors that result from our voting than has been recognized, especially by those who are more inclined to make a hasty pudding of criticism than to publish their own list of red or black sayings.

It is undoubtedly evident from what I have said that the Seminar does its work collaboratively. The scale and complexity of the task calls for the learning and insight of many, and the face-to-face discussion and debate has often affected the outcome. The result is not a winner-take-all list of the true and the false, but a report of the degree of consensus the Seminar reached in which every scholar's vote is represented.

It may not be quite so apparent that the Seminar's work is also ecumenical: participation is open to any scholar who has the requisite competence to do historical research in Christian origins, is prepared to put her views on the table, and who values the collaborative outcome of the Seminar's work highly enough to have his own views bettered in open argument or be found after the vote among the minority on a given issue.

This calls for scholars whose sense of self-importance is under control.

Luke Johnson, author of *The Real Jesus* and one of the Seminar's most self-assured critics, supposes that many of the "Rules of Evidence" in *The Five Gospels* are not really criteria that enable one to distinguish what Jesus said from what others said for him or about him. They are just assumptions that fit a vision of Jesus the Seminar already had in mind before we even looked at the evidence. So what the Seminar claims as the result of research can only be called a charade.

The fact is we began our work with rules of evidence that had been refined by decades of earlier scholarship and were already widely used by critical scholars. We revised and expanded those rules as we went along in ways suggested by the nature of the evidence. While the result is admittedly not quite a thing done on earth as it is in heaven, it is nevertheless the most comprehensive and nuanced compilation of rules of evidence currently available. So the criteria we used were either inherited from reliable earlier scholarship or resulted from our examination of the evidence; they did not predetermine our assessment of the evidence. Rather than merely pretending to do research as a way of advancing our predetermined opinions, as has been alleged, many of us found that the research challenged our opinions and persuaded us to change our minds.

To date, the Seminar has collected and examined all of the sayings attributed to Jesus in the extant ancient sources up to about 300 C.E. and considered how likely or unlikely it is that they can be traced to the Jesus of history. No previous study has been similarly comprehensive either in collecting this evidence or in assessing its historicity. We published a report of this six year long study in *The Five Gospels* in 1993.

We have recently completed a similarly comprehensive study of Jesus' deeds and the events of his life. We expect that a report on this second phase of the Seminar's work will be published in 1997, entitled, *The Acts of Jesus.*

We have also produced a new translation of the gospels that we call Scholars Version, which appears both in *The Five Gospels* and in *The Complete Gospels.* Scholars Version seeks

both to use fresh, contemporary language and to be faithful to
the sense and style of the original Greek text. It does not defer
to or privilege the traditional renderings of liturgy, Catechism,
or the history of theology. The aim is to produce a translation that addresses today's North American reader as directly
as the first readers saw or heard themselves addressed. Work on
a Scholars Version translation of the Pauline and other early
Christian letters is in progress.

We have also succeeded in calling the attention of the
media and the public to the significance of scholarship on the
historical Jesus and on the gospels, and in the process have
enabled some of our critics to enjoy even more than their
allotted fifteen minutes of fame. One can only wonder how
they could have managed without us.

The aim of the first two stages of the Seminar's work was
to create a database. We sifted the evidence to identify which
pieces of information transmitted in the ancient sources are
likely to be authentically historical. In *The Five Gospels* we
published the database of Jesus' sayings. But some of our critics
have treated this database of Jesus' sayings as if it were intended
to be the Seminar's finished profile of Jesus. The Seminar, it is
said, presents a Jesus who is merely a talking head, or a Jesus
who is not Jewish, or a Jesus who is a frivolous smart alec
whose sayings have been emptied of their religious meaning. All of these attempts to find the Seminar's prefabricated
profile of Jesus surreptitiously hidden between the lines of
The Five Gospels or lurking mostly behind the lines—visible
only in occasional remarks in the commentary, or betrayed by
the Seminar's use of the Gospel of Thomas as a source, or in
the Seminar's judgment that the eschatological sayings in the
gospels are the comments of Jesus' followers, not of Jesus himself—all of these are apparitions that live only in the irritated
imaginations of some of our critics; but none of these apparitions has ever attended a meeting of the Seminar.

The Seminar unanimously agreed in a formal vote that it is
necessary to give attention to Jesus' deeds and the events of his
life if we are to gain a view of him as a figure of history. Once
you know that, the apparition of Jesus the talking head van-
ishes, unless, of course, a belief in such phantoms renders one

impervious to the facts. The other apparitions likewise disappear when they are brought into the light of day.

Let me emphasize by saying one more time that what the Seminar has been doing since its inception is compiling a database. We did not directly address the question of what kind of historical figure can be recognized in these data until we had finished compiling them. Using the database to draw profiles of Jesus is the challenge that the Seminar is only just now taking up.

It must be acknowledged, of course, that the move from data collection to historical reconstruction is not simply a matter of moving materials developed in the isolation of a decontaminated laboratory to an outdoor construction site. The rules of evidence used to collect data do predispose the interpretation of data and can do so in substantive ways. Critics of the Seminar are right when they recognize this. But often their anticipation of what this must necessarily lead to runs their train of thought off the track of substantive criticism into the ditch of self-serving polemic. Substantive criticism usefully advances learning; ill-tempered polemic only clouds the issue, and may even be the means of avoiding the issue.

The collection and interpretation of data are interrelated, but they are not synonymous. Pieces of evidence do not connect themselves. The pattern of which they are the expression is not a foregone conclusion. The data will disclose their meaning only if they are insightfully read.

The Seminar has now begun the third phase of its work, the challenge of reading the data, because if we did not, one could well ask why we went to all the trouble of collecting them in the first place. The whole point of collecting the data was to create as complete and as carefully examined a body of evidence as possible to provide a basis for the attempt to gain a glimpse of Jesus as a figure of history. What can be expected as the result of this third phase of the Seminar's work? The first clue about what one can expect is given in the name we have chosen for this third phase. It's in the plural: profiles. We will probably agree about some important elements of the profile of this historical figure, and it will be interesting for us to discover what they are. In this part of the result of phase three we

will be continuing one of the original aims of the Seminar: to
discover what degree of consensus there is among us as critical
scholars about the Jesus of history. The second thing that we
will discover is what we disagree about in drawing a profile
of Jesus and why: on the basis of what data, by drawing what
inferences, according to what insight or paradigm. Here we
can clarify matters of interpretation by keeping each other
open and honest about what we are doing and why. For scholarship on the historical Jesus this could prove to be the most
important result of all.

And one thing more: having implicitly made the claim that
gaining knowledge about the Jesus of history makes a difference, we are under some obligation now, it seems to me, to say
what that difference is and what that difference might mean to
anyone who treasures our religious heritage. We have already
begun to debate the question of how to do this with integrity.

Concluding Comment

In his 1983 Jefferson Lecture in the Humanities, an annual
event sponsored by the National Endowment for the
Humanities, Jaroslav Pelikan, Sterling Professor of History at
Yale, says, "Tradition is the living faith of the dead, traditionalism is the dead faith of the living" (65). That aphorism offers
a pertinent way of expressing what is at stake in the question
of the historical Jesus. "It is traditionalism that gives tradition
such a bad name," Pelikan remarks. "The reformers of every
age, whether political or religious or literary, have protested
against the tyranny of the dead, and in doing so have called for
innovation and insight in place of tradition" (70). Indeed, the
capacity for insight that is the spiritual endowment of every
human being must not and ultimately cannot be suppressed by
an authoritarian past. Tradition and insight are often in tension, however, rather than simply in opposition, a tension that
is "an ineradicable element of the tradition itself," as Pelikan
puts it (73). Tradition, after all, has its origin in insight and the
preservation of that originating insight is tradition's paramount
purpose. The tension between original insight and the forms
of its transmission accounts for the fact that "during much of

our history, [new] insight has often come through the recitation and rearrangement of materials from tradition," as Pelikan notes. It is much to be hoped that the renewed quest of the historical Jesus will serve no lesser end.

Chapter Three

The Making of The Five Gospels

Marcus J. Borg

As the first systematic and collaborative examination of the totality of the Jesus tradition ever undertaken, the Jesus Seminar is unprecedented in the history of scholarship. The course for this undertaking was set by founder Robert Funk at the opening meeting in March of 1985:

> We are about to embark on a momentous enterprise. We are going to inquire simply, rigorously, after the voice of Jesus, after what he really said. In this process, we will be asking a question that borders the sacred, that even abuts blasphemy, for many in our society. . . . Our basic plan is simple. We intend to examine every fragment of the traditions attached to the name of Jesus in order to determine what he really said—not his literal words, perhaps, but the substance and style of his utterances. We are in quest of his voice, insofar as it can be distinguished from many other voices also preserved in the tradition.

A primary step in that quest was the preparation of a new translation of the gospels. Known as the Scholars Version and

The Fourth R 7,5 (September/October 1994), pp. 3–8

done by a group within the Seminar, it sought to express the particular characteristics of the original languages in contemporary English.

The Scholars Version enables the English reader to hear familiar texts in fresh ways. Words can become old through habituated hearing. In particular, the words found in sacred texts easily acquire a revered status, which obscures the tone of the "street Greek" often found in the gospels. Because the Scholars Version makes available nuances of meaning not found in most translations, it is a useful complement to other versions of the gospels, especially for study purposes.

With the Scholars Version in hand, the Jesus Seminar assessed the degree of scholarly consensus about the historical authenticity of each of the sayings attributed to Jesus, in the New Testament and other early Christian documents written before the year 300. Over one hundred scholars were involved during a six year period. When that task was completed, we decided to undertake a second phase. This examination of the historicity of events associated with the life of Jesus in the gospels—the "deeds tradition"—is now ongoing.

Seminar Fellows reflect a spectrum of contemporary scholarship. Requirements for membership are formal, not ideological: typical qualification is a Ph.D. in relevant areas of gospel research. Most are professors in universities, colleges, and seminaries. Almost all are from North America, due to the practicalities of travel and distance. Most are men, because there are relatively few women working in the discipline.

Fellows also reflect the spectrum of mainline Christian denominations. Though the Seminar has no connection to any church body, and no records of church membership of Fellows is made, my impression is that there are about equal numbers of Catholics, protestants, and non-religious. Many are ordained. A few Jewish scholars have been involved.

Though fundamentalist scholars are welcome, none have become members, presumably because their understanding of Scripture as a "divine product" makes the activity of the Seminar unnecessary and irrelevant (and perhaps even blasphemous). A few Southern Baptist scholars took part until pressure from within their denomination forced them to withdraw.

During the years when the sayings were being considered, thirty to forty Fellows were typically present at the twice-yearly meetings. Each meeting focused on a particular collection of sayings (for example, the parables, the Kingdom of God, the Sermon on the Mount). Papers were written and circulated beforehand, so meeting time would not be spent reading them. Rather, the meetings were dominated by discussion of the sayings, one-by-one, until nobody had anything further to say that would count one way or the other toward the authenticity of the saying.

The Colors of the Gospels

Discussion of the sayings was followed by voting. This voting, and the colors associated with it, has generated both publicity and controversy from the beginning.

Fellows of the Seminar voted on whether they thought a particular saying goes back to Jesus himself by casting one of four differently colored beads into a ballot box. A red vote means, "I think these are the authentic words of Jesus"; pink means, "A close approximation of what Jesus said"; gray means, "Not Jesus' words, though they may reflect his ideas"; and black means, "Inauthentic; definitely not spoken by Jesus." A weighted average of the votes—and a color—was assigned to each saying.

The Jesus Seminar is aware that one cannot actually determine what Jesus said by voting. Voting cannot settle historical questions, and majorities (even consensus majorities) are sometimes wrong. Moreover, we know that the votes on some of the sayings would likely be quite different ten or twenty years from now (just as the votes on some would have been different twenty or thirty years ago). What the voting does do, however, is to measure current scholarly opinion. It discloses the degree to which there is presently a consensus within this group of scholars.

The colors provide a visual representation of this consensus. Red and pink both indicate a quite solid positive consensus. A few Fellows voted black most of the time, with a gray vote being a major event for them. Many voted gray much of the time, only occasionally venturing a pink or red vote. Therefore, for a saying to receive a weighted average in the pink range indicates a considerable degree of positive consensus (and even more so in the case of red). Similarly, a quite strong negative consensus is indicated by black.

Compared to the other color indicators, gray is a more mixed and ambiguous category. Given that the color scheme corresponds to a descending scale of historical authenticity, it is natural to think of gray as pointing to a moderately negative consensus (as "probably not"). However, gray frequently functioned as an "I'm not sure" vote; indeed, one of its agreed upon questions in the Seminar was "well, maybe."

Gray may thus point to uncertainty. Or, rather than meaning "the consensus is gray," gray may point to absence of consensus, indicating that the distribution of votes was "all over the place." Thus rather than meaning "Jesus probably didn't say this," gray often means that this is a saying about which there is considerable uncertainty and/or division in the discipline.

Gray material in *The Five Gospels* is perhaps best understood as being in a "historical suspense account": The verdict is not clear. Gray may also signal likely directions of research in the next several years, as scholars turn their attention to this material about which no reasonably firm scholarly judgment has yet formed.

Illustrations

A few significant examples will help illustrate the work and thought underlying *The Five Gospels*.

The Gospel of Thomas

One striking feature of *The Five Gospels* is that it contains five gospels rather than the familiar four. The fifth gospel is Thomas, unknown until 1945 when it was discovered in Egypt, buried in the ground with fifty other early Christian manuscripts. For the study of the teachings of Jesus, it has turned out to be the most significant manuscript discovery ever made.

Thomas is a "saying collection" containing 114 sayings attributed to Jesus. They fall into roughly three categories. A

significant percentage resemble passages also found in the synoptic gospels. Sayings in a second category strike one as "odd"
and suggest that the tradition behind Thomas was developing
in a particular direction with a distinctive perspective. A third
category includes sayings not found in the other gospels, but
which sound as if they could come from Jesus.

The scholarly analysis of Thomas took several decades.
A foundational question concerned its age and whether it
was dependent on or independent from the other gospels
(that is, whether the author of Thomas knew one or more
of the other gospels as written gospel, or whether Thomas
represents an independent stream of oral tradition). By the
1980s, a generally (though not universally) accepted twofold
conclusion was being reached: Thomas is independent of the
canonical gospels, and contains some material as early as anything in them.

The Jesus Seminar built on this history of Thomas research
and contributed significantly to it with its consistently careful
consideration of Thomas texts. Our deliberations seemed to
confirm the conclusion that Thomas is independent, and some
of it is very early. In some cases, a saying from Thomas was
found to be earlier than a similar saying within the canonical
gospels. Thus, the parables of the mustard seed, wedding ban-
quet, and wicked vineyard tenants in Thomas were voted to be
more original than their parallels in the synoptic gospels.

Likely to be of greatest public interest are a few sayings
found only in Thomas to which the Seminar assigned pink
votes. If the Seminar is correct, these are authentic words of
Jesus unknown for over 1500 years, until their rediscovery in
this century. They include two short parables, both of which
refer to "God's imperial rule" (the phrase used in the Scholars
Version for the more familiar "Kingdom of God"):

The Empty Jar (Thom 97)
God's imperial rule is like a woman who was carrying
a jar full of meal. While she was walking along a distant
road, the handle of the jar broke and the meal spilled
behind her along the road. She didn't know it; she hadn't
noticed a problem. When she reached her house, she put
the jar down and discovered that it was empty.

The Assassin (Thom 98)
The Father's imperial rule is like a person who wanted
to kill someone powerful. While still at home, he drew
his sword and thrust it into the wall to find out whether
his hand would go in. Then he killed the powerful one.

A third pink-coded passage from the Gospel of Thomas is a
provocative saying about the "imperial rule of God." The disciples ask Jesus when the kingdom will come, thereby implying
that it is a future reality which is not yet here. Jesus responds
(Thomas 113):

It will not come by watching for it. It will not be said,
'Look here!" or 'Look there!' Rather, the Father's imperial rule is spread out upon the earth, and people don't
see it.

In more familiar language, the passage affirms that the kingdom of God is already here, spread out upon the earth—only
people typically do not have the eyes to see it.

Eschatology ("Last Things")
The Seminar consistently voted as "black" all sayings in which
Jesus is reported to have spoken of "the end of the world," a
last judgment, the coming of "the Son of man," or his own
second coming. For scholars, this result is news because it con-
stitutes a thorough rejection of the eschatological consensus
that had dominated Jesus scholarship for much of this century.

The consistent black votes on second coming and last judgment texts will probably surprise the larger Christian and non-
Christian public, though many are unaware that mainstream
scholarship thought Jesus expected an imminent eschaton. The
Seminar does not think Jesus spoke of his own second coming.
Rather, it sees language about a second coming originating in
the early community after Jesus' death.

Also in black are all passages that speak of an eternal judgment: the threats of being cast into a furnace of fire, or into
the outer darkness where there will be weeping and wailing
and gnashing of teeth, or of a harvest of wheat and a burning
of weeds. So is the famous last judgment parable about the
sheep and goats, the former to be given everlasting life and

the latter condemned to everlasting fire. As a group, we do not think Jesus' message was about how to gain heaven and avoid hell.

The Kingdom of God

Our negative verdicts about an imminent eschaton and last judgment are also reflected in our voting on kingdom of God texts. Texts which speak of the kingdom as a future reality soon-to-come (which were one of the pillars of the eschatological understanding of Jesus) are black. These include Mark's well-known summary of the message of Jesus (Mark 1:15), which I quote first in the more familiar language of the Revised Standard Version and then in the language of the Scholars Version:

> The time is fulfilled, and the kingdom of God is at hand; repent, and believe in the gospel. (NRSV)

> The time is up; God's imperial rule is closing in. Change your ways, and put your trust in the good news! (SV)

On the other hand, we regularly voted pink on sayings and parables which speak of the kingdom as present, such as Luke 17:20–21, Thomas 113, and Luke 11:20 = Matt 12:28. According to the Seminar, Jesus thought of the kingdom of God as a present reality, all around us, but difficult to discern.

The Lord's Prayer

To the surprise of the Seminar, our voting on the Lord's Prayer attracted more media headlines than any other vote taken: news of the vote appeared as a front-page story in over one hundred Sunday newspapers. We concluded that Jesus did not teach the Lord's Prayer as a connected whole, but that parts of it probably go back to him.

Does the Lord's Prayer go back to Jesus? No. Do portions of it reflect prayer concerns of his? Yes. The basis for this conclusion was threefold.

First, the Lord's Prayer appears in three different terms in early Christian documents: in Matt 6:9–13, Luke 11:2–4, and in Didache 8:2–3 (a collection of teachings attributed to the twelve disciples, probably written around the year 100). If one thinks the whole of the prayer goes back to Jesus, one is immediately faced with the question, "Which whole?"—that is, which version? Clearly, they cannot all go back to Jesus. Once one sees the three forms, it seems clear that the Lord's Prayer is part of the community's developing tradition rather than going back in one of its present forms to Jesus himself.

Second, we were skeptical that Jesus taught his followers a rote prayer to be memorized. The Seminar thought it more likely that the early movement created the Lord's Prayer for use in community worship. Matthew's formal liturgical opening, "Our Father who art in heaven" seems clearly to reflect such use.

Third, the common elements in the three versions seem early, and may very well reflect "prayer fragments" going back to Jesus himself. These include the introductory use of the informal and intimate "Abba" (Aramaic for "Papa," an unusual, even if not unique, way of addressing God), and four petitions: the hallowing of God's name (as Abba!), the kingdom petition, bread for the day, and the forgiveness of debts.

Parables and Aphorisms

Two categories of material consistently received the greatest number of positive votes. Many of the parables of Jesus in their earliest form are in red or pink: the Good Samaritan (Luke 10:30–35), the Dishonest Steward (Luke 16:1–8a), Workers in the Vineyard (Matt 20:1–15), the Lost Coin (Luke 15:8–9), the Lost Sheep (Luke 15:4–6), the Corrupt Judge (Luke 18:2–5), the Prodigal (Luke 15:11–32), and others. On the other hand, some familiar parables are in gray or black: the Rich Man and Lazarus (Luke 16:19–31), Wheat and Weeds (Matt 13:24–30), Wise and Foolish Virgins (Matt 25:1–13), Sheep and Goats (Matt 25:31–46).

Also in red and pink are many of the aphorisms of Jesus, short memorable sayings which colloquially can be described as "great one-liners." Eight of these received the highest number of red votes (thus the highest weighted average) of any votes taken. About fifty more aphorisms are also red or pink.

Topping the list of these red-colored aphorisms, in descending order of votes: turn the other cheek (Matt 5:39 = Luke

6:29a), coat and shirt (Matt 5:40 = Luke 6:29b), blessed are the poor (Luke 6:20), go the second mile (Matt 5:41), love of enemies (Luke 6:27b), woman leavening bread (Luke 13:20–21 = Matt 13:33), emperor and God (Mark 12:17b = Thom 100:2b), and give to beggars (Matt 5:42a = Luke 6:30a).

The earliest forms of the parables and aphorisms are thus seen as the bedrock of the Jesus tradition. Both are wisdom forms of speech, and taken together they point to Jesus as a "wisdom teacher." About this, there is the greatest consensus within the Jesus Seminar.

Chapter Four

The Road to the Jesus Seminar

Perry V. Kea

As a fellow of the Westar Institute's Jesus Seminar, I have had many opportunities to discuss the historical Jesus with interested audiences. While these audiences are usually enthusiastic to learn, most are not aware of the larger intellectual context for the work of the Seminar. So I have prepared the following overview of that context. Please note, this is far from a full accounting of the history of scholarship on the historical Jesus. I have provided some bibliography at the end of this essay for those who wish to know more.

Born of the Enlightenment

The quest for the historical Jesus was a product of the Enlightenment. The Enlightenment was an intellectual movement in eighteenth-century Europe and North America that promoted reason as the sole standard for establishing matters of truth. The ramifications were enormous. The political underpinnings of the American and French revolutions were

The Fourth R 18,1 (January/February 2005), pp. 9–16

established by Enlightenment figures (for example, Locke and Voltaire). The scientific method was born out of the Enlightenment. The privileging of reason over other modes of knowledge (such as tradition) meant that history was brought "down to earth" so to speak. The reasons why things happened in the past had to be sought within the space-time continuum of human life without appeals to divine agency. Just as the scientist could not appeal to supernatural forces to explain natural events, so the Enlightenment historian could not claim that historical events happened because "God so willed it."

When scholars informed by the Enlightenment considered the figure of Jesus in the gospels, they began to ask if the claims made for Jesus could be supported by rational evidence or arguments. So began the quest for the historical Jesus.

The Early Quest

The writing of history begins with sources of evidence. For the study of Jesus, the primary sources are the written gospels. In the late eighteenth and early nineteenth centuries historians began examining these written records for their evidentiary value. It quickly became apparent that the Gospels of Matthew, Mark, and Luke shared numerous similarities. How was one to explain these similarities, such as common content, sequence, and wording (often *verbatim*)? Thus was born the "synoptic problem." Various theories were developed to explain the similarities as well as the differences between the synoptic gospels —Matthew, Mark, and Luke. By about the late nineteenth century, a consensus had developed around the view that Mark's gospel was the earliest of our extant gospels and that it was used as a source by the authors of Matthew's and Luke's gospels. Furthermore, since Matthew and Luke shared material not found in Mark's gospel, it was hypothesized that they had access to a second source, dubbed Q (for *Quelle*, the German word for "source"). While there were (and are) alternative explanations for the synoptic problem, one of the firm conclusions from this early period in the quest for the historical Jesus was the recognition that the Gospels of Matthew, Mark, and Luke are literarily related in some way. All historical Jesus research is informed by this fact.

The nineteenth century also produced numerous "lives" of Jesus. The classic treatment of this period of scholarship is Albert Schweitzer's *The Quest of the Historical Jesus*, published in German in 1906 and in English in 1910. Schweitzer not only provided penetrating critiques of many of these "lives," he championed a view of Jesus that had only recently come onto the stage of scholarly debate. That view held that Jesus was an apocalyptic prophet. As Schweitzer interpreted the evidence from the gospels, he argued that Jesus expected God to bring the present age of unrighteousness to an end by some kind of divine miracle. As a result, Jesus urged people to prepare for this imminent event. He taught an "interim ethic," a way of living until God intervened to replace this age with the age to come, the kingdom of God. Frustrated by the non-occurrence of God's intervention, Jesus went to Jerusalem to force the issue. As Schweitzer famously expressed it, Jesus threw himself on the wheel of history by challenging the religious authorities in Jerusalem. In the process, Jesus was crushed by that wheel.

While there were dissenters, by the time the First World War had ended, the view that Jesus was some kind of apocalyptic preacher was becoming the majority view of scholars. It was also becoming apparent that if this view was correct, the Jesus of history was not going to provide a very adequate basis for traditional Christian claims about him.

Between the World Wars

The period just after World War I saw a change of focus in historical Jesus studies. German scholars Rudolf Bultmann and Martin Dibelius began applying the method of form criticism to the gospels. The dominant question for historical Jesus research in the nineteenth century had been the issue of the earliest written sources about Jesus. Form critics recognized that before anything was written down about Jesus, the memories of what he said or did were preserved and transmitted orally. Drawing on studies of folklore, form critics demonstrated that the oral traditions about Jesus behaved in some predictable ways. Sayings of Jesus or stories about him tended

to conform to specific types or forms. By identifying the different forms and describing their generic features, form critics
believed they were gaining a glimpse into the traditions about
Jesus before they were written down. It was recognized that
the various forms were assembled by the first writer(s) of the
gospel; that is to say, the order and sequence of the episodes
in the gospels is artificial. This meant that the chronological
sequence of the events of Jesus' life as related in the gospels
could not be taken at face value.

Among biblical scholars and theologians, interest in the
historical Jesus significantly waned. Bultmann accepted the
view that Jesus was an apocalyptic figure, but he argued that
Christian claims about Jesus were not, and should not be,
based on the life or teaching of the historical Jesus. Although
Bultmann wrote his own historical reconstruction of the message of Jesus, he argued that the Jesus of history was of little
importance for New Testament theology, which was based
on the resurrection experiences of the earliest community of
believers. As Bultmann famously put it, the crucified Jesus rose
again in the preaching of his early followers. Early Christian
theology flows from this preaching, not from what Jesus himself taught. Consequently, fewer scholars devoted their energies
to reconstructing the historical Jesus and, instead, spent more
energy on the theological activity of early Christianity. This
period in scholarship is sometimes called the period of the
"No Quest."

The New Quest

After the Second World War, Bultmann continued to be influential. A substantial body of his publications was translated
into English and so reached a wider audience. Furthermore,
Bultmann trained a number of scholars who carried forward
his projects. While there had been critics of Bultmann who
argued that the Jesus of history was compatible with traditional
Christian claims (for example, Joachim Jeremias in Germany
and C. H. Dodd in England), it was Bultmann's own students
who renewed the quest for the historical Jesus. In a famous
essay, Ernst Käsemann articulated the position that while we

could not expect the historical Jesus to mouth the precise claims made by his later followers, Christian theology had a right to expect that the mission and teaching of Jesus be consistent with the claims made about him after his resurrection. It is well to remember that this "New Quest" for the historical Jesus was motivated by the theological aspirations of (mostly) Protestant scholars.

Gunther Bornkamm's *Jesus of Nazareth* is an excellent example of a German New Quest study. James Robinson's *A New Quest of the Historical Jesus* (1959) put an American face on the discussion. In the 1960s and early 1970s, British born, German trained Norman Perrin taught in the United States and published several influential works on Jesus.

Yet, the 1970s and early 1980s were relatively quiet on the historical Jesus front. In part this was because the academic study of the New Testament and early Christianity was branching out from historical and theological studies to include literary and ideological studies. The attention of many scholars turned away from the quest for the historical Jesus.

New Manuscripts: The Dead Sea Scrolls and Nag Hammadi

The seeds of renewed interest in the historical Jesus were planted with new manuscript discoveries. The study of early Judaism and early Christianity were enhanced significantly by the manuscripts known as the Dead Sea Scrolls (1947) and the Nag Hammadi codices (1945). As the initial manuscripts from the Dead Sea were published in the 1950s, new studies were generated. The scrolls demonstrated that Judaism in the late Hellenistic and early Roman periods was more diverse than had been imagined previously. Before the Dead Sea Scrolls, New Testament scholars had usually described the Judaism of this period through the lenses of the New Testament and early Rabbinic literature. Study of the scrolls helped scholars to see that the way in which many New Testament documents characterized Judaism was biased and that this bias reflected the occasionally polemical and antagonistic situations that existed between early Christian and Jewish communities. Likewise, the corpus of Rabbinic literature was late and reflected the ascendancy of one particular Jewish group. Other Jewish voices were marginalized or suppressed. The Dead Sea scrolls represented a Jewish community that pre-dated the rise of Christianity and Rabbinic Judaism.

In broad terms, the scrolls appear to have been produced by a sect of Jews whose leaders were dissident priests. The Dead Sea community seems to have been comprised of Jews who had withdrawn from the Temple in Jerusalem because of disagreements with other priests who controlled it. This group established a small community by the shores of the Dead Sea that was consumed by a desire to maintain a high level of ritual and moral purity. Moreover, the people of this community developed an apocalyptic theology. They prepared for a great cosmic battle between the sons of light and the sons of darkness. They produced interpretations of Jewish scripture that reveal their own particular concerns and peculiarities. The community at the Dead Sea was obviously and thoroughly Jewish. Yet that community of Jews disagreed strongly with all the other Jewish groups of their day. The Dead Sea scrolls made it abundantly clear that one could no longer talk about "normative Judaism" at the time of Jesus. Judaism was far from being a monolithic religion. To be sure, there were common beliefs and practices, yet Judaism was as diverse then as it is now.

The discovery of the Nag Hammadi texts had a similar impact on our understanding of Christianity. The documents in the Nag Hammadi collection were obviously produced by Christian communities that did not fit the traditional, orthodox description of early Christianity. These texts, mostly produced in the second and third centuries of the common era, revealed a diverse side of Christianity that had only been hinted at before. Several of the documents found at Nag Hammadi were gospels. The most famous of these is the Gospel of Thomas, well known to those who have followed the work of the Jesus Seminar. The availability of new documents purporting to contain material about Jesus stimulated scholarly interest. Might some of these materials provide historically reliable information about Jesus or his teaching? As early as 1962, the noted German scholar, Joachim Jeremias, was suggesting that some sayings in the Gospel of Thomas merited consideration as authentic parables of Jesus.

Parables and Aphorisms

In an ironic way, a scholarly shift away from history to literary criticism would significantly enhance our historical under-standing of the role played by parables and aphorisms in Jesus' teaching. In 1964 Amos Wilder (brother of the famous play-wright, Thornton Wilder) wrote *The Language of the Gospel: Early Christian Rhetoric.* Wilder showed that how something was expressed contributed to its meaning. It had been thought by many New Testament scholars that the content of a mes-sage could be extracted from its literary form, as if the liter-ary form were the "husk" and the message were the "kernel." Because of Wilder that view began to change. Two important studies on Jesus' parables and language appeared in the mid-1960s and one on Jesus' aphorisms in the mid-1970s: Dan Via's *The Parables: Their Literary and Existential Dimensions* (1967), Robert Funk's *Language, Hermeneutic, and Word of God: The Problem of Language in the New Testament and Contemporary Theology* (1966), and Robert Tannehill's *The Sword of His Mouth* (1975). These works demonstrated that the aesthetic dimension of Jesus' language was not merely decorative or ornamental, but essential to the communication of his message. While these works were concerned to examine Jesus' speech forms for their literary qualities, they also had the effect of demonstrating that the author of these parables and aphorisms (namely, Jesus) had a rather subversive or unconventional view of reality.

While the majority view still held Jesus to be an apoca-lyptic preacher, these studies on Jesus' parables and aphorisms prepared the way for a new appreciation of the wisdom ele-ment in Jesus' message. In the 1970s and 1980s, other scholars pursued these issues. For example, John Dominic Crossan's *In Parables: The Challenge of the Historical Jesus* (1973) and *In Fragments: The Aphorisms of Jesus* (1983) explored the interac-tion between Jesus' language and the socio-cultural realities of

Jesus' day. Bernard Brandon Scott began working on a comprehensive analysis of the parables that culminated in 1989
in his *Hear Then the Parable*. Sixteen years later Scott's book
is arguably still the best commentary on the parables in any
language.

The renewed appreciation of Jesus' skill with parables and
aphorisms prepared the way for a different evaluation of his
alleged apocalypticism. This turn toward the Jewish wisdom
tradition and away from the Jewish apocalyptic traditions was
reinforced by several studies in the late 1960s and 1970s on
the "Son of Man" (translated "son of Adam" in the Scholars
Version) expression. It had long been recognized that Jesus
rarely applied titles to himself in the synoptic gospels, except
for the title "Son of Man." Scholarship had long grouped the
Son of Man sayings into three categories:

1. present activity of the Son of Man (for example, the Son
   of Man has nowhere to lay his head; the authority of the
   Son of Man to forgive sins)
2. the impending suffering of the Son of Man (the Son of
   Man must suffer, die, and be raised from the dead)
3. the future appearance of the Son of Man from heaven.

There was broad and longstanding consensus that the suffering Son of Man sayings were creations of the early church,
especially those sayings framed as predictions. Their specificity
was judged to be due to the fact that the church knew the
particulars of Jesus' suffering and death and so formed these
sayings as a way of making sense of Jesus' mission.

It was noticed that in the present Son of Man sayings the
expression "Son of Man" could be understood not as a title,
but as a Jewish idiom for "human being." For example, Psalm
8:4 had declared "What is man that thou art mindful of him,
and the son of man that thou dost care for him?" (Revised
Standard Version) and the prophet Ezekiel is frequently
addressed as "son of man" (translated "mortal" in NRSV). So
by about 1980, many scholars were convinced that the expression "Son of Man" in this group of sayings should be understood in this generic sense.

Proponents of the view that Jesus was an apocalyptic preacher cited the heavenly Son of Man sayings. In these sayings, the expression "Son of Man" seemed to function more as a formal title. Moreover, several of these "Son of Man" sayings seemed to make a distinction between Jesus and the future Son of Man ("Whoever is ashamed of me and my words in this sinful generation, of him will the Son of Man be ashamed when he comes in the glory of his holy angels"). Bultmann had accepted Schweitzer's argument that Jesus was an apocalyptic preacher, but had modified this by suggesting that Jesus did not think of himself as the future, heavenly Son of Man. Rather, Jesus' mission and message was to prepare people for the heavenly appearance of this Son of Man figure.

However, several works in the 1960s and 1970s argued that these heavenly Son of Man sayings were creations of the early church. In a series of essays, Norman Perrin demonstrated how this might have developed. By the early 1980s, Marcus Borg was floating "A Temperate Case for a Non-Eschatological Jesus" (read "eschatological" for "apocalyptic"). When the Jesus Seminar began its work, the time was ripe for a full debate. Whether Jesus was or was not an apocalyptic figure depended largely upon whether one judged the heavenly Son of Man sayings to derive from Jesus or from the early church. But it was also the case that the work on Jesus' parables and aphorisms were pointing to the importance of the Jewish wisdom tradition for determining what kind of Jew Jesus was.

Archaeology and the Social Sciences

Finally, interest in the historical Jesus was facilitated by the utilization of explanatory models from sociology, anthropology, and archaeology. As New Testament scholarship experimented with literary methods in the 1960s and 1970s, it also looked to the social sciences for tools that could help make fuller sense of these first century documents. The differences between first-century Mediterranean cultures and twentieth-century industrial societies compelled scholars to look for models that more nearly matched the first century. For example, cultural anthropology provided studies of demon possession in so-called "Third World" societies that closely resembled the gospel accounts of Jesus' exorcisms. The Jesus Seminar's deliberations on these stories were informed by such anthropological studies.

One of the criticisms of the Seminar that people sometimes share with me is its conclusion that there is a historical core to the exorcism stories. These people complain that the Seminar is not being skeptical enough: demons don't really exist. How can there be such a thing as an exorcism? Such a complaint is typical of a twentieth (now twenty-first) century western mind. But cultural anthropology has demonstrated that belief in evil spirits is not only common throughout human cultures, but that it is tied to demonstrable social factors. In cultures where women's roles are severely restricted, the incidence of claimed demon possession is much higher for women than for men. In societies where males are politically suppressed, the claimed demon possession rate is higher for them. These kinds of studies, combined with studies of the social, economic, and political systems of the first century, have helped make sense of the exorcism stories. While we twenty-first century westerners may not believe in demon possession, first-century people did. They were not merely superstitious; such stories reveal much about the way these people experienced their lives. Likewise, in that culture, a person like Jesus with a proven track record as an exorcist would have been very popular.

Sociology and anthropology have contributed many other ways for understanding the lives of the people who produced the gospels (and the other documents of early Christianity). The work of archaeology has revolutionized our understanding of the context of Christian origins. While there had been important excavations in ancient Israel, including first-century sites, throughout the twentieth century, the significance of excavations in Jerusalem and Galilee conducted between the 1950s and the early 1980s was just beginning to be realized. It had long been assumed that Jesus' home region of Galilee in northern Israel was less exposed to the cultural forms of

Greece and Rome than Jerusalem and southern Israel. The historical stereotype of first-century Galilee was that it was a rural backwater, off the beaten tracks of Greco-Roman influence. Archaeological excavations in Galilee changed that view. One of the sites that attracted the attention of archaeologists was Sepphoris. Never mentioned in the New Testament, it is now recognized as a very important site. Destroyed by Herod the Great, it was rebuilt by his son, Herod Antipas, in the second decade of the first century C.E. Excavators discovered a thoroughly Romanized city. As Antipas' administrative capital for Galilee, Sepphoris served as a kind of showplace. It signaled Antipas' support of and compliance with the Roman Empire and provided cultural and civic opportunities for the ruling elite. One of the most spectacular finds at Sepphoris was a Roman style villa decorated with beautiful floor mosaics. What was particularly instructive about Sepphoris was the fact that it was only about four miles from Nazareth, the home of Jesus. Jesus' father, Joseph, is described in the gospels as a *tekton*, usually translated as "carpenter." That is a proper translation of the term, but *tekton* has a broader range. It refers to artisans with some kind of skill. Presumably, when Sepphoris was being built in the teens of the first century C.E., it provided employment opportunities for skilled laborers. Jesus would have been in his teens when the construction of Sepphoris began. Though it cannot be proven, scholars speculate that Jesus learned and applied the artisan skills of his father on the construction projects of Sepphoris.

Even apart from the question of Jesus' involvement in the construction of Sepphoris, the excavation revealed a revolutionary fact: Galilee was exposed to Greco-Roman urbanization to a far greater degree than previously thought possible. This realization meant that historians of the gospels would have to re-imagine the social, economic, and political realities presupposed by those stories.

The Time Was Ripe

I suspect that if Robert Funk had never convened the Jesus Seminar in 1985, the current renaissance in historical Jesus studies still would have occurred. The new discoveries, methods, and studies of the 1960s, 1970s, and early 1980s were bound to stimulate new efforts to locate Jesus of Nazareth within the historical circumstance of first-century Jewish Palestine. The Jesus Seminar had the good fortune to come along at an auspicious time. My own personal experience may serve to illustrate the appeal the Jesus Seminar afforded.

I completed my Ph.D. at the University of Virginia in 1983, having written a dissertation on the aphorisms in the Sermon on the Mount. Dan Via, whose work on the parables was mentioned earlier, was my principal advisor. In 1975, as a college undergraduate, I had written a senior thesis on the Son of man sayings in which I had concluded that the heavenly Son of man sayings were creations of the early church. So when the opportunity to attend a meeting of the Jesus Seminar came to me in 1987, I went. At that first meeting someone recognized that I had done my dissertation on aphorisms. So it was suggested that I join a group working on the aphorisms of Jesus (at that time, there were several different groups working on various projects). Before my first meeting was over, the chairperson of the aphorisms group, John Kloppenborg, had persuaded me to take on a paper for the next meeting of the group. I continued as a member of the Jesus Seminar because I enjoyed the work and the camaraderie of the Fellows and Associates, but also because of the opportunity to soak in the new information and lines of study that I have briefly described above. I know that my teaching has been informed by the archaeological and manuscript finds, the explanatory models of cultural anthropology and sociology, and the literary studies of early Christian traditions. New Testament scholarship is a richer and more diverse field than ever before. By 1985, the time was ripe for a fresh approach to the quest for the historical Jesus. Robert Funk's idea to convene a Jesus Seminar was right for the time.

Chapter Five

How Did We Get Here?

Looking Back at Twenty Years of the Jesus Seminar

Bernard Brandon Scott

T he Jesus Seminar has celebrated its twentieth anniversary, completed its major project, and suffered the loss of its founder, Robert Funk, and of one of its pillars, Daryl Schmidt. The Seminar is now embarking on a new project on Christian Origins. This is an appropriate time to look back and evaluate the Seminar's work.

Retrospect

This retrospective on the Jesus Seminar and its first report, *The Five Gospels,* will not be an effort to engage or respond to our critics. As my personal view, this evaluation concerns how I have put together what we, the Seminar, have accomplished. I make no pretense that this is an objective, detached history of the Seminar. It is an insider's view of what happened, a participant's view.

I was, to quote a famous text, there "in the beginning." I was actually there even before the beginning when Robert

The Fourth R 19,5 (September/October 2006), pp. 3–10

Funk called together a group of scholars to begin planning for the Jesus Seminar. His vision was simple: send out a general invitation to scholars to participate in a project that would color code the gospels like the old red-letter Bibles, only his plan would be to print in red only the words that in the scholars' judgment Jesus actually said. Funk thought this project would take two to three years at most.

That was Funk's plan; of course, it turned out very differently.

Before I continue this story, let me address what I take to be Funk's primary goal in proposing the Seminar. There has been much speculation and surely he and the scholars gathered for the project had many reasons for joining together. But Funk has been clear about his overall goal. The title of the magazine of Westar Institute boldly proclaims the goal: *The Fourth R*. Funk viewed this project as part of a desperately needed program in religious literacy. The general public in his judgment demonstrated dangerous illiteracy about matters religious, especially the Bible. The historical scholarship on the Bible was almost unknown among the general public. To name biblical illiteracy as dangerous was certainly a prophetic move on Funk's part, for the fourth R seems as much in decline in American culture as the other three Rs.

We should evaluate *The Five Gospels* by how well has it contributed to public literacy about the Bible in general and about Jesus in particular.

Funk thought this project would be simple because scholarship had been working on the issue of the historical Jesus for more than 150 years, at least since Strauss's *The Life of Jesus* (1838). So all that was needed was to summarize this 150 years of work, get the scholars to vote yea or nay, and print the result. What could be easier?

The fact that it did not turn out to be so simple only confirmed Funk's opinion of the contrariness of scholars.

The first two meetings were devoted to methodology. The first meeting was at Berkeley, California (March 1985) and the second at St. Meinrad, Indiana (October 1985), where I was teaching at the time. Eugene Boring presented a paper on the methodology for discerning the authentic words of Jesus.[1]

While Boring's essay was a strong survey of the traditional criteria, as Bob Dylan might have said, "the times, they were a-changin'." The criteria were themselves shifting. Why the shift was occurring involves following a complicated trail.

Two important agreements resulted from these first two meetings:

- The scholars decided that two colors were insufficient.
- We could reach no agr eement on method.

Also, we managed to vote only on the Beatitudes. So what Funk thought would take two to three years was now a year old, and only a tiny amount of material had been voted on. He must have been in despair.

Good reasons compelled those two conclusions and they have had a profound effect on the Seminar's direction. The fellows quickly decided that an either/or, red or black, judgment did not represent the state of scholarship. Two colors made it appear considerably less ambiguous than the state of affairs actually is. The either/or position is at heart a fundamentalist position. Scholarship almost always makes things more complicated because it elucidates more possibilities. Since informing the public was our primary goal, we needed a more sensitive instrument. So we decided to move to four colors.

Red – Jesus actually said it.

Pink – Jesus probably said it.

Grey – Jesus probably did not say it.

Black – Jesus surely did not say it.

We never actually agreed on what the color scheme meant. *The Five Gospels* suggests (pp. 36–37) two other ways to understand the colors, both of which differ from the way I understand them. The greatest difference on the colors' meaning has to do with grey. For some it indicated a saying was even less likely to be from Jesus than a pink saying. For these folks

---

1. Boring's paper represents the culmination of a long tradition of debate about criteria that had reach a clear formulation in the work of Norman Perrin.

grey was less than pink. In the metaphor commonly used at
the time, while grey sayings could be included in the database
of Jesus sayings, they would be employed with caution. For
others, grey was a lack of certainty that it was not black. For
these, grey was less than black.[2] This differing point of view
eventually would have profound implications on the Seminar's
direction.[3]

The colors provided a visual and intuitive clue to their
meaning. While in a perfect world the colors would have exact
meanings, the intuitive nature of the colors reminds the user of
The Five Gospels that votes represent a range of positions—not
a single absolute position. The votes for the *Five Gospels* were
not written on stone, but in pencil on paper ballots.

The most important aspect of the voting was that it forced
scholars to make decisions. Without such discipline, it is too
easy to engage in a sleight of hand, in which we know a saying
is not from Jesus, but go ahead and use it anyway as somehow
suggesting what Jesus was about. For a classic example of this
procedure, consider Mark 1:15: "The time is up: God's imperial rule is closing in. Change your ways and put your trust in
the good news." This saying has often been used as a summary
of Jesus' teaching about the kingdom of God, even though it
was clearly composed by the gospel's author, not Jesus.

The second important non-conclusion from the Seminar's
first two meetings was that after an extensive methodological
discussion on the use of criteria for determining the authentic
sayings of Jesus, we agreed not to follow a common method.
This is not quite as chaotic as it sounds, since we all agreed
on the canons of scholarship, but there was no real agreement
on which criteria were most important or how the various
criteria were to be evaluated. The principal division within
the Seminar was between those who favored the criterion of
dissimilarity and those who favored multiple attestation. The

---

2. For further analysis of the Seminar's ambiguities about the grey
vote, see Robert J. Miller, *The Jesus Seminar and its Critics,* pp. 52–53.

3. I often suspected that this differing perspective on gray/black
represented an unspoken theological divide between the Fellows.
The more conservative theologically trusted the gray material. As my
summary above indicates, I belong to the less-than-black school.

criterion of dissimilarity, which had dominated the scholarship prior to the Seminar, seeks those aspects in which Jesus is different from expectation, whether Jewish or Christian. Multiple attestation builds its case based upon independent occurrences of items, downgrading those that occur only once. John Dominic Crossan was one of the most important advocates within the Seminar for the importance of multiple attestation.

This lack of uniformity in method was in my judgment a virtue. Scholarly papers were presented and debated on each item to be voted. So the issues were always carefully and fully discussed and the vote represented the common wisdom of scholars who have considered and debated the evidence. By "common wisdom" I mean the considered judgment, with each scholar using his or her experience and expertise as a scholar to weigh the evidence. As Mark Allan Powell has noted, "The harmony of so many usually independent voices is precisely what demands that attention be given to this chorus of scholars."[4]

In the Beginning
Is the End

The early membership of the Seminar had a great deal to do with how the picture of Jesus that emerged from the voting developed. I do not want to slight any scholars who were active in those early days, but there were certain groupings that were important. Scholars from a variety of specializations came to the table. In my mind the following groups turned out to be critical:

- Parables (John Dominic Crossan, Robert W. Funk, Bernard Brandon Scott)
- Apocalyptic (Gene Boring, Adela Collins, John Collins)

---

4. *Jesus as a Figure in History,* p. 78. A few pages after this statement, Powell remarks, "What marks the Jesus Seminar as unique—probably the *only* thing that marks them as unique—is that they are a group. . . . Only seventy-four scholars consented to place their names on that volume. Still, that is seventy-three more names than are associated with any of the other positions described in this book" (p. 81).

- Q (John Kloppenborg, Stephen Patterson, James M. Robinson)
- Gospel of Thomas (Harold Attridge, Ron Cameron, Karen King, Stephen Patterson, James Robinson)
- Social World (Burton Mack, Vernon Robbins)

These five topics represent a rearrangement or reconfiguration of New Testament scholarship on the issue of the historical Jesus. Scholarship—and by extension the Jesus Seminar—does not begin with a blank slate. Scholarship is cumulative—we do not reinvent the wheel each time we start, although there is often a conceit in our writing that implies this. While scholarship is not "creation out of nothing," neither does it develop in a straight line. It advances and retreats and new methods wash over from other scholarly disciplines. New Testament study is not isolated from the scholarship in other disciplines and has always reflected what was going on in other historical disciplines. When the Jesus Seminar met for the first time, we were not starting from scratch. The strength of the Seminar was that it was a group of scholars representing a variety of methodological perspectives. The group was committed to three points:

- Critical Method
- Discussion and argument
- Voting

The first two are common to the scholarly enterprise. The third, voting, is not; and its democratic spirit has offended the elitist inclinations of some scholars. But the point of the voting is a not a winner-take-all approach to truth: it is to show a reader the range of positions within scholarship. It makes evident the unity and fissures within scholarship, something seldom put on public display.

Social World

Traditionally the quest for the historical Jesus has been divided into stages. After WWII form criticism and its offshoot, redaction criticism, dominated historical Jesus research and synoptic criticism. Form criticism, as practiced by Rudolf Bultmann, studied individual pieces (forms or types) of the tradition, in order to identify the contexts for their uses (a concept scholars refer to with the German phrase *Sitz im Leben)* within early Christianity. Redaction criticism, building on form criticism, focused on the creative contributions of the individual evangelists in order to distinguish their particular theologies from the traditions about Jesus each of them inherited.

New elements were complicating the picture. The methodologies of sociology and anthropology under the heading of social world studies were making their impact felt in New Testament studies. This required a focus on the social situation in a broader sense than form criticism had in its interest in *Sitz im Leben.* For example, comparative sociology shows that the issue of social formation or group allegiance is a concern not of the first generation but later. Therefore the parable of the Wheat and Tares (Matt 13:24–30), which addresses the concern about distinguishing "true" from "false" disciples, was judged not to be from Jesus but of a following generation. This type of argument built upon an understanding of how social formation takes place provided an important criterion and a new element in the debate.

Q-Gospel

John Kloppenborg and James M. Robinson put Q, the Synoptic Sayings Source, at the center of the debate. In his then recently published dissertation, *The Formation of Q,* John Kloppenborg divided Q into three stages. The original stage was a wisdom collection, in which the kingdom is viewed as a present reality. In the second stage an editor adds apocalyptic elements foretelling imminent judgment upon those who rejected the preaching of Jesus and the Q community.[5] Kloppenborg clearly demonstrated that these were editorial or redactional additions. This analysis of Q has proven to be the most powerful and convincing to date. Significantly, the first

---

5. See *The Five Gospels,* p. 136–37, for good discussion of "wisdom" and "apocalyptic."

two stages of Q are pre-70 C.E. Kloppenborg's work showed that Q was a fascinating window onto a group of Jesus folk in Galilee in the 50s and 60s. No canonical gospel can claim this, since they all were composed after the traumatic events of the destruction of the Temple in 70.

These Q studies became important in the Seminar's considerations for three reasons:

- Q was pre-70.
- Q was compiled in Galilee in Greek.
- At its earliest stage Q was a wisdom, not apocalyptic, text.

Q becomes (along with Paul) our best evidence for what was happening in the early Jesus movement prior to the Temple's destruction. The Seminar privileged pre-70 material, acknowledging the great impact of the destruction of Jerusalem and its Temple on the development of both Judaism and Christianity. This is not so much the privileging of Q over the narrative gospels as it is a recognition of the historical chasm created by the Temple's destruction. Q therefore came to play a large role in our understanding of the historical Jesus.

My major criticism of *The Five Gospels* is that it was not *The Six Gospels*. The Q Gospel should have been the first gospel in *The Six Gospels*.

Gospel of Thomas

Also among the membership of the Seminar were a number of scholars who were doing pioneering and original work on the Nag Hammadi library of Coptic texts. For the reconstruction of early Christianity, this buried library of a Coptic monastery will turn out to be more important than the much more famous Dead Sea Scrolls. Nag Hammadi offers us a view of Christianity outside the emerging canon.

Since its discovery the Gospel of Thomas has fascinated those working on the historical Jesus. Joachim Jeremias acknowledged its importance in the sixth edition of his *Parables of Jesus* (German edition 1962). And yet a number of problems persist in dealing with the Gospel of Thomas.

- A Coptic translation of Greek text

The Greek text exists only in fragments. The only complete text of Thomas we possess is a Coptic translation of a Greek original. That means we have little history of Thomas's transmission. Imagine what we might think of the Gospel of Mark if it existed in only one manuscript in Coptic. Would it occur to anyone that it was the first gospel, the source of Matthew and Luke?

- Date of Composition

Dating has bedeviled the interpretation of Thomas because, unlike the synoptic gospels which make reference to the destruction of the Temple, the Gospel of Thomas makes no apparent reference to any obvious event that might allow an approximate dating. The form of Thomas, a sayings gospel, similar in form to Q, might indicate an early dating. Furthermore, it seems that Thomas, like Q, developed in stages. The Seminar's debate about the date of Thomas, and especially our presentation of that debate to the public, would have benefited had the question been brought to a vote. Then our public could have seen the range of debate and discussion on the date of Thomas within the Seminar.

- Gnostic or Wisdom?

Scholarship on Thomas has debated whether it is Gnostic. This often strikes me as scholarly name calling. Label something as Gnostic and it does not have to be taken seriously. The Gospel of Thomas is about as Gnostic as the Gospel of John. The Seminar in its wisdom set this issue aside and simply dealt with individual sayings in Thomas.

- Independent of or dependent on the synoptic gospels?

The Gospel of Thomas is clearly related to the synoptic tradition, but that does not mean that it depends on any one (or more than one) synoptic gospel. The Seminar opted for the position that Thomas was independent of any synoptic gospel for two primary reasons.

1. Argument from Order

   The order of the sayings in Q is derived from a comparison of the order in which they appear in Matthew and
   Luke. While Luke appears to have followed the order of
   Q more closely, Matthew too preserves the basic order
   of Q. A comparison of the order the sayings in Thomas
   and the synoptics reveals no pattern of dependence. This
   would argue strongly for Thomas's independence from
   the synoptic gospels.

2. Redactional Interference

   If the Gospel of Thomas was dependent on one or all
   of the synoptics, we would expect Thomas to betray
   redactional elements from the synoptics. This does not
   happen in any systematic way. In my judgment this is the
   strongest indication of Thomas' independence from the
   synoptic gospels.

If the Gospel of Thomas is independent of the synoptic
gospels, then in effect the canon is breached. The canon no
longer has a privileged position in the reconstruction of the
historical Jesus or early Christianity. The title of the report of
the Jesus Seminar, *The Five Gospels,* clearly indicates that the
canon no longer has a privileged place in establishing historical understanding. It may well have a privileged place in the
theological discussion, but even that might be revisited.

From the beginning the Seminar decided to cast its net
wider than the canon to include all the material attributed
to Jesus in the first three centuries. Constantine declared
Christianity a tolerated religion in 313, so this seemed a reasonable cut-off date. We did this on good historical grounds.
We agreed to examine all the data and not allow ourselves to
be prejudiced against non-canonical material.

What does the Gospel of Thomas add to our knowledge
of the historical Jesus? Nothing spectacularly new. Its significance lies in how it illuminates existing evidence. Before the
discovery of the Gospel of Thomas, the form "sayings gospel"
was a theory; after its discovery it was a fact. This makes Q
much more important and credible because the existence of

Thomas proves that early Christians wrote some gospels composed solely of sayings, with no story elements. The Gospel of Thomas also rearranges the data. Some sayings that are singly attested in the canonical gospels have multiple attestation thanks to the Gospel of Thomas (as we will see below in the case of Luke 17:20–21).

Wisdom vs. Apocalyptic

Was Jesus a preacher of apocalyptic doom or did he make his point with subversive wisdom? Since Albert Schweitzer's *The Quest of the Historical Jesus* (1906), the consensus of scholarship had maintained that Jesus preached the imminent coming of an apocalyptic kingdom of God. But there were important dissenters. Many (e.g., Bultmann and Jeremias) had proposed a both/and (or yet and not yet) solution—the kingdom was both present and future. In an even smaller camp C.H. Dodd proposed that Jesus' eschatology was realized—the kingdom was present.

For reasons mostly accidental, the Seminar began with the parables of Jesus, at the meeting in Redlands, California (March 1986), the Seminar's third meeting. There was little discussion about what the parables meant. Most issues were of a formal nature. The debate did not start off by asking whether a parable was from Jesus, but whether it was redactional, i.e., the product of the evangelist.

The parable of the Rich Man and Lazarus (Luke 16:19–31) is an interesting example of the Seminar's process. In the history of scholarship, a number of scholars had questioned the parable's ending (vv. 27–31). I was in the last stages of writing *Hear Then the Parable* and volunteered to produce an essay surveying the various positions taken on the historical character of each parable for the Redlands meeting.[6] In my paper I argued that the conclusion of the parable was a Lucan construction.[7] The Seminar agreed and voted this section of the parable black—definitely not from Jesus.

---

6. "Essaying the Rock."

7. Following Dominic Crossan, *In Parables,* pp. 66–67.

The first part of the parable also presents a number of problems. It is the only parable that mentions the afterlife in such vivid detail and that uses a proper name, Lazarus. These two items in themselves should raise formal doubts about the parable. Furthermore, the theme of the rejection of the rich is a well known Lucan theme, almost a fingerprint. Robert Tannehill, a prominent Lucan scholar, persuaded the Fellows that Luke had constructed the parable and so, despite my analysis of the parable arguing that it was from Jesus, they voted gray. Significantly the Fellows were making their decisions based on well established formal criteria, not on whether they thought Jesus preached a future or present kingdom, or whether he was oriented to apocalyptic or wisdom. Those issues did not come up in these early stages of the debate.

Parables that are found only in the Gospel of Thomas had a difficult time in making the cut. This indicates that the Seminar was more conservative methodologically than is generally supposed.[8]

The real debate concerning Jesus' eschatology came not during discussion of the parables, but at the Seminar's fourth meeting at Notre Dame (October 1986). At the Redlands session on the parables Fellows had established Jesus' primary form of teaching to be parables and aphorisms, but the issue of their relationship to the kingdom of God had not been dealt with. For the Notre Dame meeting, important papers were prepared by Burton Mack and Karen King. Mack argued that Mark turned the kingdom wisdom language into apocalyptic language. Mack's argument parallels Kloppenborg's argument concerning Q: that the final version of Q is an apocalyptic redaction of an earlier collection of wisdom teachings. Two sayings can illustrate the issues involved in the debate.

Luke 17:20–21

When asked by the Pharisees when God's imperial rule would come, he answered them, "You won't be able to

---

8. The Empty Jar (Thomas 97) is an interesting example. It was considered three times by the Seminar, the first two times receiving a gray vote, only barely getting a pink vote on the third try. See the commentary on this in *The Five Gospels,* p. 524.

observe the coming of God's imperial rule. People are
not going to be able to say, 'Look, here it is!' or 'Over
there!' On the contrary, God's imperial rule is right there
in your presence."

This saying is probably the strongest, most obvious one in support of the non-apocalyptic Jesus. It clearly rejects signs and
predictions into the future and instead focuses on the present.
It paradoxically introduces a collection of sayings with a strong
future, apocalyptic outlook. One could dismiss this saying as a
Lucan creation attempting to mitigate the strong future ori-
entation of the material that follows (Luke 17:22–37), except
that the saying does not employ typical Lucan vocabulary. The
clincher in the argument is that a parallel saying appears in the
Gospel of Thomas (Thom 113:2–4). Since the Seminar had
adopted a position supporting the independence of Thomas
from any synoptic gospel, Thomas 113 counts as an independent attestation of this saying, which means that neither Luke
nor Thomas composed it. The Seminar's vote was pink for
both the Thomas and Luke versions. Now the significance
of the independence of the Gospel of Thomas becomes evident. While it adds little new information, it can significantly
change how the data are assessed.

Mark 1:15
The time is up: God's imperial rule is closing in. Change
your ways and put your trust in the good news.

This saying is part of Mark's introduction to his gospel. It
clearly is a summary statement of what Mark takes to be Jesus'
message. While most scholars have acknowledged that Mark
composed it, many have argued that it represents Jesus' true
message. Since the saying is clearly Mark's summary, it cannot be from Jesus. So the strongest vote those supporting the
authenticity of the saying could argue for was a gray. But the
vote turned out to be black. The Seminar rejected the saying
as evidence for the historical Jesus.

Thus Luke 17:20–21 and Thomas 113, and not Mark 1:15,
became the determining sayings that grounded the Seminar's
position that Jesus was a preacher of the present kingdom of
God. The voting points to a major issue that emerged from

those early votes. The evidence for an apocalyptic Jesus cannot be found in the primary level of the sayings tradition. One now begins to see the importance of Kloppenborg's argument about the structuring of Q—his conclusion that apocalyptic sayings were added to the wisdom sayings of Q. This makes the wisdom sayings primary. Furthermore, since Mark edited the kingdom sayings towards apocalyptic, the evidence for an apocalyptic Jesus becomes very thin, to the point of disappearing.

In the history of the Seminar, the 1986 Notre Dame meeting was a watershed. Those who supported the apocalyptic view of Jesus found themselves in the minority and so began to drift away from the Seminar. That was unfortunate, but it would not have changed the Seminar's direction. What was moving the Seminar was not presuppositions about who Jesus was, but new configurations of both the evidence and methods that were reshaping and continue to reshape New Testament scholarship. Critics of the Seminar routinely accuse its members of having prior theological preferences for a non-apocalyptic Jesus and of voting based on this prejudice rather than on an honest assessment of the evidence. Curiously, that attack is never accompanied by serious arguments against the authenticity of Luke 17:20–21 or Thomas 113 or for the authenticity of Mark 1:15. Because of the mix of membership in the Seminar and new methods employed by those members, the votes of the Seminar were ahead of the curve, forging a new paradigm for study, a paradigm not anticipated by the Seminar members, but forged in the voting process itself.

Evaluation

My evaluation of the Seminar's accomplishments comes in two parts. First I will deal with how participation in the Seminar has affected me as a scholar; then I will make what I hope is a more "objective" evaluation.

The Personal Level

The discussions of the Fellows forced me to change, to shift my view of Jesus' "eschatology." Those discussions were so important, so difficult, and so penetrating that I have decided

never to use to the word "eschatology" because I am afraid
that it is a weasel word, a word without a precise meaning and
so a commentator can make it mean whatever is needed. I
found those discussions at Notre Dame a personal trial because
I had to decide among the positions of long-standing friends.
Not an easy task.

Since my first book, *Symbol-Maker for the Kingdom,* I had
been in the doubting column about apocalyptic in Jesus'
teaching. I had been able to find evidence for an apocalyptic
future only in the Lord's Prayer and so I had remained in the
"yet and not yet" position. Still, the more I worked with the
evidence, especially the parables and Q, the more I became
convinced that for Jesus the kingdom of God remained a present reality.

A second important lesson I learned from the Seminar is to
be clear about what I can argue comes from Jesus and what
are the limits of debate. For my part I have decided that one
should begin with the evidence—what did Jesus say and do
—and that we should answer that question as much as possible on formal grounds. Others have decided that they need
to start with the context in which Jesus fits. Both Marcus Borg
and Dale Allison are good examples of this method.[9] Borg
adopts the spirit filled charismatic model from Huston Smith,
while Allison adopts an apocalyptic model. My problem with
this method is that selection of the data should come first—
determine what it is, then discover what pattern emerges. They
use their model to select the data. This puts the cart before the
horse in my judgment

Finally, the Seminar developed a collaborative model. This
has been difficult for scholars in the so-called soft sciences,
although it is standard in the hard sciences. We New Testament
scholars are used to working in isolation. Submitting one's
work to a common discipline is difficult. But collaboration
produces a richer product than any individual can produce.

---

9. In "Jesus Was Not and Apocalytpic Prophet," Marcus Borg
acknowledges that he agrees with Allison's "emphasis on the central
importance of 'paradigm' through which we see the traditions about
Jesus" (p. 33).

Overall Evaluation

From the beginnings I had my doubts about this "red letter
thing." Not having been raised Protestant, red letters did not
have the symbolic power for me that it had for other Fellows.
Nevertheless I think *The Five Gospels* and its companion
volume *The Acts of Jesus* are very important and original pre-
sentations. Their true strength is the clarity of presentation.
This clarity is dependent not only on the four-color scheme,
but also on the summaries of the Seminar's discussions. These
summaries enable a reader to understand the positions that
were presented. The volumes also indicate the voting that
determined the colors. A reader can judge the validity of the
Fellows' arguments, as well as learn whether the votes spread
across a spectrum or were clustered together. In a sense this
is free market scholarship, with no intervening authority. The
reader gets to see the arguments, the votes, and she can make
up her own mind as to whether the scholars got it right.

The inclusiveness of the texts used to form the database
is a critical element. The inclusion of the Gospel of Thomas
indicates that history should not be determined by theological
(that is, canonical) assumptions.

There are several important weaknesses to what we
accomplished. Minor inconsistencies occurred in the voting.
Frequently this was determined by who showed up for the
debate and voted. In no case do I think these are serious or
even contradictory. These are probably inevitable in a project
of this duration which involved the number of folks that it did.

As noted above, the first report should have been entitled
The **Six** *Gospels,* and not *The Five Gospels.* Q and its reconstruction played a major role in the Seminar's discussions. That
should have been represented in our report by presenting a
reconstruction of Q and its color coding. *The Five Gospels* is
still more bound to the canon that it cares to admit.

A major problem with a color coded gospels is that it can
lead to a view that the gospels tell only about the historical Jesus or that their value is only to be determined by how
historically accurate they are. This is one major and important
criterion, but it is not the only way to understand the gospels.

For instance, Mark invents the gospel story, the narrative outline. From the point of view of history, that narrative outline is
a fiction. Mark uses a travel narrative, a common form in the
ancient world at least since Homer sent Ulysses on his voy-
age of self discovery. So from a historical point of view, much
of Mark can be dismissed. But that would be a grave mistake.
Mark fashions Jesus' story into a meditation on power, especially imperial power. He rejects power over others in favor of
the power of the loss of life, of service. Imperial power leads to
crucifixion as a way to maintain that power. But Jesus' crucifixion leads to service for others, to life. In this day of imperial
ambitions, I would hate to forfeit Mark's gospel by retaining
only what is historical.

A second major problem is that understanding the historical Jesus is not a straightforward task. In the best of all possible worlds one could simply select the data and then decide
whether it comes from Jesus. But this is not really possible.
Even fundamentalists cannot do this, since fundamentalists
must always impose from outside the text their model for
understanding it. (The *Left Behind* series makes a great example
of this because it imports into the text a panoply of modern
notions, especially concerning the United Nations, that were
impossible in biblical times.)

Historical scholarship is not a straightforward exercise, but
is much more circular. One almost has to know everything to
know anything. For example, to know what is redactional in
a given gospel, one has to have a very thorough understanding of that particular gospel in comparison with other gospels. Thus the arguments put forward by the Fellows imply a
whole history of early Christianity and the culture of which it
was a part. That historical context at times is made evident, at
other times implied. This critique is implied in every historical explanation. Understanding history is always like a series of
Chinese puzzle boxes. There is always another box inside the
last one you opened.

The strength of *The Five Gospels* and *The Acts of Jesus* is
their clarity of presentation. It makes available to the reader
a vast range of information that has been sorted and debated

by a diverse group of scholars. The reader can see at a glance
the range of positions. As a force advancing literacy about the
Bible, it has surely raised the level of debate.

Chapter Six

The Jesus Intervention

Ruth Schweitzer-Mordecai

The Jesus Seminar is receiving a lot of criticism these days. Many critics simply disagree with some of the scholarly conclusions reached by the Seminar. But others see it as a threat to what has been held sacred and inviolate in the church, or as an attempt to destroy Christianity. The work of the Jesus Seminar, when viewed from the perspective of family systems theory, can be compared to an intervention in a family system.

An intervention is usually made in order to confront someone in the family who is a practicing alcoholic or addict, with the hope of creating change in the person and the family system. For the Jesus Seminar, "family" is the institutional church that is confronted with the threat of change. Typical dynamics of the process of family intervention can be found in the work of the Jesus Seminar:

- The people who make the intervention are involved meaningfully in the life of the addict or system.

The Fourth R 8,3–4 (May/August 1995), pp 3–6

- They list facts about specific behaviors that have caused concern over the years and present them in a non-judgmental fashion.
- The tone of the meeting is one of deep concern.
- Data presented are specific and descriptive of events which have happened or conditions which exist.
- Evidence is presented in explicit detail to show that reality is not what the person has believed it was.

It is the purpose of an intervention to create a crisis. If there is heated reaction to the intervention, it means it is effective. In a crisis, there is a window of emotional vulnerability in which it is possible to have greater openness to change in individuals and in the system.

The Jesus Seminar addresses two aspects of the Christian system: (1) publicly telling a family secret in order to encourage open dialog about scripture, and (2) modeling a collegial, rather than hierarchical way of operating. The heated reaction to the work of the Jesus Seminar is, for some, a crisis response to the threat of change to the existing Christian system.

Telling the Family Secrets

The first aspect of the system in which the Jesus Seminar calls for change is the public telling of family secrets. A common metaphor for family secrets is that there is an elephant in the living room, that everyone avoids and no one mentions. In this case, the elephant is scholarly thinking about the historical Jesus. Though biblical criticism has been taught in seminary for years as part of the training for church leaders, most Christians are not aware of it, nor of the techniques available to scholars, nor the conclusions that scholars commonly draw.

In families, certain members, often the parents know the family secrets. Scholars who teach in academic institutions are like older children in a family who have been sent away to receive an education, but then are told not to share any concealed information that would disturb the family stability.

In his discussion of the impact of family secrets, Edwin Friedman describes how they confuse or stop the general flow of communication. Friedman points out that more significant than the content of the secret are the ramifications of their existence for the emotional processes of the entire family (pp. 50–57). Some of these are:

1. Those "insiders" (who attended seminary) are better able to communicate with one another than those "outsiders" (who did not attend) about any issue, not just the secret, causing unnecessary estrangement.

2. Secrets distort perceptions and generally function to keep anxiety at higher energy levels. When secrets are revealed, *despite initial upset,* the anxiety level of the family generally decreases. This is particularly true if the family continues to work at the issues that then surface, issues that often had precipitated the forming of a secret. The formation of a family secret is always symptomatic of other things going on in the family. People more often keep secrets to spare their own feelings than to protect others. The chronic anxiety of secrets kills.

3. The ultimate proof of the function and the power of secrets within a family is that when they are revealed, more change usually takes place throughout the entire system than could have been attributed solely to the content of that secret.

Triangles

Secrets create and perpetuate triangles. A triangle arises when two people do not communicate directly with each other, but instead use a third person as a go-between. In this case, the triangle prevents direct communication between a member of the congregation and Jesus or the scriptures (Friedman, pp. 52–59).

The secret of historical scholarship about Jesus is kept by church leadership and passed on only in seminary to the insiders. Church leaders triangulate in the "lay person's" relationship with the scriptures, Jesus, and ultimately with God. One effect of this triangle is that clergy are expected to be God-like, with no visible human limitations and failings. When the triangle is eliminated, people in the congregation, appropriately informed, become responsible for their own faith and their own relationship to God. That allows members of the clergy to become human once more.

Growing Up

Keeping this Christian family secret also forces people to assume the role of children. The issue here is about growing up. In a sense it is about accepting that we can't go home to the womb; we must go home to ourselves, where our true family resides, including God. To do that, we are helped by learning the family secrets.

Secrets always support the status quo. They are never on the side of challenge and change. Secrets are very serious stuff.

Much of the critical uproar about the Jesus Seminar concerns the content of what is publicly said regarding such volatile issues as the virgin birth, the resurrection, and Jesus' atonement. When I first attended seminary I learned that the historical accuracy of these events had been questioned for years. I was shocked and very disturbed. I went through a time of anger at not having been given this hidden information. Ultimately, this knowledge propelled me into a re-examination of my faith and beliefs. That experience led me to what I now value as a far greater freedom, to follow my own individual spiritual path within the Christian community or, if I should so choose, outside of it.

Protecting the System

What is new about the Jesus Seminar is not the scholarship but the arena for scholastic discussion. The Jesus Seminar is not just telling the family secrets, it is yelling them, going out of the way to attract media attention. This can be likened to a family in which the parents (church leadership) want parental control and the adult children (scholars) want to be treated as the adults they are. By telling the family secrets in a loud voice, the Jesus Seminar is behaving in a way that typically triggers a family crisis. As any family therapist knows, a family crisis can be the beginning of a very healthy process of change. But it is also my experience that family therapy can be one of the most devastating forms of therapy. I have great compassion for anyone involved in that process. The precipitation of a crisis is a painful time, and there is the risk of unknown results to the system. But the potential is equally great.

According to family systems theorists Michael Kerr and Murray Bowen, "The goal of unearthing a secret is to address the relationship processes that created and perpetuated the secret" (308). In this case, one reason for keeping the secret is to contain Christianity in a hierarchical structure. If only the elite (those who attend seminary) know of critical biblical scholarship and some of its conclusions, then the "adult children" in the family remain children, with neither the appropriate authority nor responsibility of adults.

Shaking Up the System

It is not easy to grow up and leave home. The existing system provides structure for everyone in it. Without structure, chaos appears and we mistakenly assume that it has no order. In my view, the most creative and valuable sense of order is that which emerges from chaos. So I welcome this shake up of a system that has become too structured, without sufficient room for individual purpose and definition. I also know what it is like to have the basic structure of my life, in terms of family and of religious belief, come apart and be in chaos for awhile before integrating in a new way. It is a terrifying process, and usually brings up great resistance. My survival instincts go on red alert. It seems to me that this is a predictable reaction to the work of the Jesus Seminar, especially because of its high visibility. It is not just a response to the content of the conclusions of the Jesus Seminar, but to the inclusive, open discussion of such taboo topics as whether Jesus believed that he was the messiah. This intervention, if it continues and is persuasive, has the potential for encouraging drastic change in the church.

Collegiality

This brings me to the second aspect of the Jesus Seminar that threatens the institutional church. In its own internal process, the Jesus Seminar models a collegial way of being in community and of coming together to accomplish tasks. Papers are invited and studied, debate is held publicly and, ultimately, a vote is taken. Associates, those interested but without academic credentials in this field, are separately asked to vote and those results are also published. In various ways, the Fellows are in frequent dialog with the Associates. There is a wide variety of viewpoints among the Fellows of the Seminar. Debate and disagreements are expected. The published conclusions do not reflect the views of any one person, and the purpose of the votes is not to establish a new creed. The threat is not about the content, provocative as it is. The threat to the system, to the ways the church has operated, is found in the process of the Seminar. It is open and collegial and, to the best of its ability, clear about any assumptions that it wishes to make as a body. To the degree that other "family" members are drawn to that model, change will result.

It is also important to note that the Jesus Seminar is addressing specific aspects of Christianity. It is engaged in a highly intellectual process focused on scripture, which is only one aspect of spirituality or religion. But it is claiming the right to engage fully in that process and debate publicly and state its findings. Because this is not the accepted process of the existing church system, it is a threat.

One premise in family systems theory is that it is possible to change an entire system, if one member of that system is willing to change his or her way of being in relation with the rest of the system. How the system will change cannot be predicted, but a change is inevitable. The threat to the system is genuine and the reaction will probably continue to intensify. It is probable that a certain amount of chaos will be felt.

I have come, reluctantly, to trust the process of entering the chaos. I discovered this one day when I fell into a river. There is, indeed, a more creative and meaningful order that presents itself if one is willing to ride the rapids to discover it. I wish us all a good ride.

Chapter Seven

Answering the Critics

A Scholar Responds to Jesus Under Fire

Roy W. Hoover

R esponses to *The Five Gospels: The Search for the Authentic Words of Jesus* have been numerous and varied, but only a few of them have been written by New Testament scholars who claim to know the truth about the historical Jesus better than do the Fellows of the Jesus Seminar. In this article, I will review one of the most recent of these.

In *Jesus Under Fire* (Michael J. Wilkins and J. P. Moreland, eds.), ten New Testament scholars have joined forces to deal with "the furor" about the historical Jesus that has appeared in the public media in recent years. At the forefront of the endeavor that has attracted such troubling public notice is the Jesus Seminar (p. 2). The contributors to this volume, eight of whom hold teaching positions at evangelical Christian seminaries or colleges, believe that the work of the Jesus Seminar is not a *search* for the historical Jesus, but an *attack* on him. Whereas the scholars of the Jesus Seminar have gone to the extreme of "denying the accuracy of the biblical portrait of Jesus found in the New Testament," the volume's editors say,

The Fourth R 8,5–6 (September/December 1995), pp. 17–20

"others have contended that the Jesus found in the Bible and
declared in the creeds of the church is the true Jesus of history" [the view shared, presumably, by the contributors to this
volume] (p. 5). Their aim in publishing the volume is to demonstrate that "the claims of radical New Testament critics like
the fellows of the Jesus Seminar are false and not reasonable
to believe in light of the best evidence available" (p. 7). I will
confine my remarks on this broadside rebuttal to the work of
the Jesus Seminar mostly to the chapter entitled, "The Words
of Jesus in the Gospels," since it most directly responds to the
report of the Seminar in *The Five Gospels.*

The author of the chapter on the words of Jesus is Darrell
L. Bock, Professor of New Testament studies at Dallas
Theological Seminary, an independent evangelical institution.
Of basic importance for the argument advanced by Professor
Bock is the distinction he makes between "the *ipsissma verba*
('his very words') and the *ipsissma vox* ('his very voice')" (p. 77)
in the report of Jesus' teaching found in the gospels. By Jesus'
"voice" Bock means both a summary of what Jesus taught and
its subsequent interpretation by those who believed in him. So
understood, Jesus' "voice" is more important than a verbatim
quotation of his words, in Bock's view, because in his "voice"
we hear what he really meant, not merely what he actually
said. Jesus' "voice" develops out of his words, to be sure; but
it is not simply identical with them. Bock puts his point this
way: "Sometimes events and sayings are understood better after
reflection than when they first took place." In such instances
the meaning of a saying or teaching can often he better
expressed in a retrospective summary than in a direct quotation, "because the events that follow it reveal its full import" (p.
81). We all know that the full truth of history is the meaning it
comes to have in retrospect, Bock says; and what is true about
history as we experience it is also true about the historical
Jesus: it is in the retrospective view of him which we read in
the gospels that we learn the truth about him.

The difference between Professor Bock's conception of
what the search for the historical Jesus is about and that
of most critical scholars, including the Fellows of the Jesus
Seminar, is apparent in his definition of Jesus' "voice." It

would be more historically accurate to call what Bock calls the "voice" of Jesus, the "voice" of the early church. It is in the early church's formulations of their faith that Bock finds the full meaning of what Jesus taught, not in a recovery of what Jesus said on his own. That Jesus meant "more" than he actually said is what his followers grasped after Easter, and this "more" is what Bock takes to be Jesus' authentic "voice." Historically viewed, what Bock claims is Jesus' "voice" is actually early Christian interpretation.

When members of the Jesus Seminar refer to Jesus' "voice," they refer to the characteristic stance and style of Jesus' teaching before Easter, not to the retrospective theological meaning conferred upon Jesus' life and teaching by his followers after Easter. Bock's definition of Jesus' "voice" refers to the early history of Christian thought, rather than to a search for the historical Jesus. His paramount interest, it seems clear, is Jesus' life's meaning, not his life history. Jesus does not speak for himself in Bock's treatment of his teaching; the gospel authors speak for him. They are the ones who most adequately know what Jesus meant.

When Bock chooses sayings material to illustrate how his approach works in the study of the gospels, in order to demonstrate the validity of his conception of history and his method of inquiry, the difference between his approach and that in *The Five Gospels* is similarly unmistakable. Bock's choices of sayings materials are all *confessional:* what t*he voice from heaven* said at Jesus' baptism, "You are my Son, the beloved; with you I am well pleased" (Mark 1:11; parallels in Matthew 3:17, Luke 3:22); *Peter's answer* to Jesus' question about who he really is, "You are the Christ" (Mark 8:27–30; parallels in Matthew 16:13–20, Luke 9:18–21); and Jesus' response to the high priest's question during his trial about whether or not he was the messiah, "I am. . . . And you will see the Son of Man sitting at the right hand of the Mighty One and coming on the clouds of heaven" (Mark 14:61–62; parallels in Matthew 26:63–64, Luke 22: 67–69).

These are the sayings that matter, in Bock's view. Even though parables and aphorisms constitute about seventy percent of the content of sayings attributed to Jesus in the gos-

pels, according to one recently published estimate, not one
of them is mentioned in this discussion of his words. In *The
Five Gospels* the first two of the sayings Bock chooses to support his claims are not color-coded at all, since they are not
sayings attributed to Jesus; the third is colored black, because
the Seminar regarded it as almost certainly the creation of the
gospel authors, not a saying of the historical Jesus. It seems
likely, on the other hand, that Professor Bock would have colored each of his three choices red, since they express what he
believes is the truth about the historical Jesus.

It is evident from his conception of how the gospels work
as accounts of Jesus' life and work, summarized above, and
from his selection of these three confessional statements as
evidence that supports his conception, that Professor Bock's
aim (and that of his colleagues who have contributed to the
volume) is to defend the gospel portraits of Jesus, not to search
for Jesus of Nazareth as a figure of history. In other words,
what interests Professor Bock and his colleagues is not the
historical figure of Jesus as he was before the gospels were
written, but the messiah and savior who is portrayed in them.
What, in their view, the Jesus Seminar denies—"the *biblical
portrait* of Jesus found in the New Testament" (p. 3, emphasis
added)—they want to defend. Their intention, in other words,
is to defend the reliability of the gospels as authoritative scriptures, not examine them as sources in which one may find
historical evidence.

Professor Bock's discussion of the criteria of authenticity ignores the fresh and nuanced presentation of these in the
introduction to *The Five Gospels* as "rules of evidence," and
resorts to older definitions of three criteria—dissimilarity, multiple attestation, and coherence. He claims that the Seminar
both misconstrues these, as he defines them, and fails to use
them consistently. Professor Bock's discussion of the criteria of
historical authenticity seems to me to be untouched by historical consciousness. Son of Man Christology together with
the idea of Jesus' death as a sacrifice for sin and a ransom for
many is the ruling criterion of authenticity for him. Historical
matters are merely aids to the vindication of this messianic

and redemptive meaning. With history thus safely subordinated to theology, it is easy for Professor Bock to see these theological themes as authentic elements of the teaching of the Jesus of history, and easy also for him to see flaws in the Jesus Seminar's methodology and assessments.

Bock's discussion of the criteria of authenticity shows that what really is at issue between him and his colleagues and the Fellows of the Jesus Seminar is not likely to be clarified by a debate about criteria. At bottom, what distinguishes the scholars of the Jesus Seminar from the scholars who have contributed to *Jesus Under Fire* is not so much different judgments about the criteria of authenticity (or "rules of evidence"), as a different conception of the meaning of authenticity. That is, what distinguishes the two books is the difference, as Van A. Harvey characterized it thirty years ago, between a devotion to the ethic of religious belief and the authority of tradition, on the one hand, and a commitment to the ethic of critical judgment and historical knowledge, on the other. Within these ethical universes both the role of the historian and the nature of historical evidence are understood differently. The former was for centuries the traditional view, according to which

> the historian's task is one of compiling and synthesizing the testimony of so-called authorities or eyewitnesses. Formerly, the function of the historian was regarded essentially as an editorial and harmonizing one. It rested on the assumption that the historian has an obligation to believe another person's report when that person claims to have knowledge of or to have observed an event. The historian is regarded as the believer and the person believed is the authority. (*The Historian and the Believer,* p. 40)

This traditional view of historical evidence and of the historian's task is continued in the work of the contributors to *Jesus Under Fire*. Their aim is to come to the defense of the reliability and historicity of the portrait of Jesus in the gospels. As the editors of the volume put it, "The authors of this volume are serious scholars deeply committed to the truthfulness and rationality of historic, biblical Christianity and the spiritual implications that follow from such a commitment" (p. 14). Here is devotion to the ethic of religious belief and to the authority of tradition in full voice.

A scholar who is committed to the ethic of critical judgment and historical knowledge, on the other hand, sees the persons whose testimony provides us with the evidence on which we depend for knowledge of the past as historical creatures whose perceptions and judgments inevitably reflect both the conceptuality and culture of their time and their own position, interests, and beliefs as participants in that world, not as authorities whose word is simply to be trusted. From this perspective, as Harvey puts it, it is the responsibility of the historian to assess the inferences and judgments made in the sources,

> to establish not only their meaning but their truth. He cannot avoid either task, for to assume that the reports mean what the ordinary reader takes them to mean overlooks the historically conditioned nature of thought. To leave them uncriticized is simply to attribute to the witness a capacity for critical judgment the historian himself lacks or is too timid to exercise.
>
> In so far then as history aspires to be knowledge, in contrast to belief, the historian must give reasons for what he asserts. As soon as the reasons are forthcoming one ceases to rely on mere authority or testimony. . . . If the historian permits his authorities to stand uncriticized, he abdicates his role as critical historian. He is no longer a seeker of knowledge but a mediator of past belief; not a thinker but a transmitter of tradition. (Harvey, p. 42)

From the perspective of a scholar who is committed to the ethic of critical judgment and historical knowledge, Professor Bock's discussion of the authentic words of Jesus is the work of a scholar who has abdicated his role as critical historian in order to mediate a traditional form of belief. What we see in his treatment of Jesus' sayings is not reason in search of historical truth, but reason claiming historical support for religious belief.

The devotion to the ethic of belief that Professor Bock exhibits in his chapter on the words of Jesus is clearly and forcefully stated by the editors of *Jesus Under Fire* (p. 7) in their introduction to the volume:

> Any religious belief worthy of the name should be accepted because we take the belief to be true and do so by the best exercise of our mental faculties we can muster. Applied to Christianity, we want to know if Jesus was really like what the New Testament says he was like. Did he say the things attributed to him in the New Testament? Was he really the only begotten Son of God? Did he actually perform miracles and actually raise people from the dead in real space-time history? Are there good reasons for thinking any of these things is true? If the answer to these questions is yes, then Jesus Christ has the right to require of us an unqualified allegiance to him. If the answer is no, then Christianity as a total worldview should not be believed or propagated.

In light of this prefatory statement of the issue, it should come as no surprise to find that the criticism of the Jesus Seminar and *The Five Gospels* offered in *Jesus Under Fire* shows us not a scholarship in command of a better knowledge of the historical Jesus, but a scholarship that is unwilling, perhaps unable, even to raise the question of the historical Jesus. This volume does show us that what is a matter of principle to those who are committed to the ethic of critical judgment and historical knowledge can be, and often is, an offense to those who are devoted to the ethic of belief and the authority of tradition. Viewed theologically rather than ethically, this might be said to be the difference between seeing revelation as history and seeing history as allegedly revelatory.

Chapter Eight

The Jesus Seminar and Its Critics

What is really at stake?

An interview with Robert J. Miller

The publication of *The Five Gospels,* reporting the results of the Jesus Seminar's search for the historical Jesus, drew the fire of critics within the scholarly guild. Among others, Luke Timothy Johnson of Emory University, Richard Hays at Duke University, Ben Witherington, Asbury Theological Seminary, as well as Howard Kee, Boston University, and Birger Pearson of the University of California, Santa Barbara (both retired); all took aim at conclusions drawn by the Seminar.

Last November Robert Miller, a long-time Fellow of the Seminar, presented his assessment of the critics and the criticism for members of the Society of Biblical Literature—the professional association for biblical scholars in America—at their national annual meeting in New Orleans. Now, for *Fourth R* readers, he looks closely at these critics and their criticisms to determine what is really at stake.

4R What does the Seminar claim?

The Fourth R 10,1–2 (January/April 1997), pp. 17–26

Miller I have never understood our claim to speak for scholars to mean that most scholars agree with our specific findings or even with all of our methods. Not even members of the Seminar agree on these. What I do understand it to mean is that the Seminar's fundamental views about the gospels—that they are not historically true in all their details; that some of the words attributed to Jesus were not actually spoken by him; that the gospels contain historical memory from before Calvary and religious interpretation from after it; that they are, to put it bluntly, a complex blend of fact and fiction; and that to discover the historical Jesus we need a critical sifting of evidence rather than theological assurances—that these views do represent the consensus among critical scholars.

This is not news to scholars, but it is to the American public. A huge number of Americans believe that inerrancy is the only legitimate approach to the Bible, that to take the Bible seriously is to take it literally. [Inerrancy is the doctrine that the Bible is completely free of any kind of error (historical, scientific, moral, or religious) ed.]. According to a recent poll, 40% of Americans believe that Jesus will return to earth in the next few decades.

Critics are correct in saying that many scholars disagree with the Seminar's results, but they do a disservice if they perpetuate the mistaken impression that doubts about the historical accuracy of significant portions of the gospels are confined to some allegedly radical "splinter group." This is important because critics assert that the Jesus Seminar is little more than a "faction" with "idiosyncratic opinions."

4R Several critics point out that members of the Jesus Seminar are "self-selected." Is the Jesus Seminar self-selected and if so, what does that tell us about the Seminar?

Miller This is puzzling. Self-selection can only be a criticism on the assumption that membership in this kind of group should not be by self-selection. How then? By invitation only? The Jesus Seminar is open to anyone with the proper academic credentials. It has no way to exclude anyone who is qualified who wants to join. What if membership was by invitation only? Would that make the Seminar more credible? And if members were not self-selected, who should do the selecting? Criticizing the Seminar because it is self-selected amounts to criticizing it for not being elitist.

4R In an article in *The Christian Century,* Luke Johnson says that members of the Jesus Seminar do not represent the "cream" of New Testament scholarship in this country, and that most of the participants are in "relatively undistinguished academic positions." How would you respond to this?

Miller Wait just a minute. Take me for example. I am not in a "relatively" undistinguished academic position. I am in an absolutely undistinguished one. I've yet to meet anyone at Society of Biblical Literature meetings who's even heard of the college where I teach. I teach eight courses a year, almost all of them introductory courses. My college grants no sabbaticals. I have very little time for scholarly research and writing. I am, in short, an academic working stiff, which makes me like most biblical scholars in this country. I am much more representative of the rank and file of the mainstream biblical scholars than highly paid professors in distinguished positions on the graduate faculties of elite universities.

4R Ben Witherington, in his book *The Jesus Quest,* criticizes the Jesus Seminar for not including fundamentalists. He alleges that fundamentalists could not participate because the Seminar's approach is biased in favor of a non-fundamentalist portrait of the historical Jesus.

Miller Actually, fundamentalists could join the Seminar if they wished, but Witherington is correct to think they would feel out of place. The only way that the absence of fundamentalists in the Jesus Seminar can be construed as a criticism of its agenda is on the assumption that historical Jesus research can be carried out on the basis of fundamentalist convictions. But obviously, if we start with the belief in the literal historicity of every verse in the Bible, we rule out, by definition, critical judgments about the historical reliability of anything in the gospels. Witherington's assumption here that an unbiased approach to the historical Jesus must include the fundamentalist perspective really amounts to a rejection of the very basis of historical-critical scholarship.

For Witherington, apparently, the quest for the historical Jesus does not question the historical reliability of the gospel material, but consists only of fitting it all into a coherent and harmonized whole. Consider one of his comments on the Jesus Seminar. Referring to the Seminar's finding that only 18% of the sayings can be confidently traced to the historical Jesus, Witherington concludes that the Seminar "rejects the majority of the evidence—82%. I will leave the reader to decide whether it is a truly scholarly and unbiased approach to reject the majority of one's evidence and stress a minority of it."

This statement implies that Witherington accepts *all* the gospel material to be evidence for the historical Jesus. Only on this assumption could he accuse the Seminar of "rejecting" evidence. Without this assumption, one could not say that the Seminar rejects any evidence for the historical Jesus, but rather that it finds only 18% of the sayings to be evidence for the historical Jesus. This is not "rejecting" evidence, it is making judgments about what kind of evidence each saying is. Some are evidence for the historical Jesus and some are evidence for early Christians who attributed their own words to Jesus.

4R Another criticism, by Richard Hays, is that most professional biblical scholars are "profoundly skeptical of the methods and conclusions" of the Jesus Seminar, which he characterizes as an "academic splinter group." What is scholarly consensus, and how important is it?

Miller I would really like to know how Hays knows this. Consensus among scholars is extremely difficult to determine with any accuracy. I have a strong impression that there are a few consensus positions among New Testament scholars: for example, the existence of Q, the priority of Mark, the pseudonymity of the Pastoral Letters. But if this claim were challenged, how would I demonstrate it?

The standard method in scholarly writing is to fill footnotes with references pro and con on a given position. But this counts only published opinions. It would be fascinating for the professional societies to poll their members on a broad range of basic questions. That would give us some hard data from which to assess where the consensus positions are.

But even this would have weaknesses. Biblical scholarship is highly specialized and so a scholar's position on an issue outside his or her area of specialization may not be all that informed. For example, some scholars who make confident claims about the Gospel of Thomas cannot read Coptic, the language in which the only extant copy of Thomas is preserved. Many of the opinions of biblical scholars are simply not expert opinions. So should we give credence only to the consensus among experts? If so, who decides who is on the list of experts? I suggest that in the absence of reliable statistical data we really don't know enough to state with any assurance at all what the consensus views are on most issues.

Why is it so important to us to claim consensus support for our positions? It's not too difficult to figure this out. We believe that scholarly consensus confers authority. And authority confers power, the kind of power all scholars crave, the power of persuasion. Especially when scholars address the public, or their students, to say that position X is the position of the vast majority of scholars, that is a power play. It says: if you don't agree with it, you're either uninformed or you're not very smart.

There is nothing wrong, per se, with power plays. But scholars owe it to themselves and to their audiences, especially to their students, to be circumspect about how they use them.

4R Some critics take a dim view of the Seminar's practice of voting on the authenticity of the sayings and deeds attributed to Jesus. What would you say, for instance, to Ben Witherington's objection that truth is not determined by majority vote?

Miller This is, of course, a red herring in that no one claims that it is. Nevertheless, those who, like Witherington, make this objection commit an inconsistency when they also try to discredit the Seminar on the grounds that its views are not shared by a majority of scholars.

Witherington's specific complaint is that "only in America where majority views are assumed to be right and where 'truth' is decided by voting could this idea of voting on Jesus have arisen." However, as *The Five Gospels* explains, the Jesus Seminar got the idea, not from American democracy, but from the practice of various Bible translation committees and from the United Bible Society's committees that vote on the critical edition of the Greek text. This practice of scholars voting on the Bible actually began in England, not America.

Luke Johnson has no objection to translation committees voting because "these votes are carried out privately." This is very revealing: the real sin of the Jesus Seminar is that it does its work in public.

4R Critics dearly resent the public aspect of the Jesus Seminar. How do you respond to charges that the Seminar is "publicity hungry"?

Miller There seems to be an assumption that academics who speak publicly about religion should keep their views to themselves because they might be unsettling to the beliefs of mainstream Americans. This assumption explains why biblical scholars have largely left it up to scientists to battle creationism in the public forum.

The very fact that journalists who cover religion could register such shock that scholars would use words like "non-historical" or, worse yet, "fiction" to characterize some gospel passages shows what a good job our guild has done keeping our secrets to ourselves. I wish that reporters who interview critics of the Seminar would ask them which items in the gospels they consider non-historical. If critics were to answer this question honestly, it would signal that the Seminar's views on the general nature of the gospels are shared by virtually all critical scholars, even though many of them disagree with the Seminar's specific results.

What if the very same people in the Jesus Seminar had carried out the very same project and come up with the very same results, but had done so in private and published the results in a specialized scholarly journal? Obviously the public would not have paid any attention, but my question is: how much attention would this project have received from scholars? I suspect, but obviously cannot prove, that the quantity of the critical response would be less and its quality better. I suspect also that the sheer nastiness of the insulting rhetoric directed against the Seminar would be much reduced.

4R One aspect of the Jesus Seminar's work that consistently attracts attention is its use of early Christian sources outside the canon, especially the Gospel of Thomas. Howard Kee called the Gospel of Thomas a "radical Gnostic reworking of the Jesus tradition." And Birger Pearson, in an article in the journal *Religion,* claims that it is "completely dominated by a type of Christianity oriented to mysticism." How do you defend the use of Thomas as a primary source for the historical Jesus?

Miller Such characterizations are surely overstated. Many sayings in Thomas have no gnostic or mystical content at all. Some of them are close parallels to their canonical counterparts.

Everyone grants that Thomas has its own distinctive theological tendencies and that it has reworked a lot—but not all—of its material accordingly. But how does this make Thomas different from any other gospel?

Isn't Matthew a thorough reworking of Mark? Isn't John's reworking of the Jesus tradition just as radical as that of Thomas? Is there some assumption by critics that Thomas' gnosticizing interpretation is so pervasive that earlier, non-gnostic, material cannot be distinguished? In fact, the redactional modifications that reflect a gnostic perspective are usually utterly obvious, almost ham-fisted, and are easily detachable from earlier material.

Within the Seminar there is consensus that Thomas is not dependent on the canonical gospels and that, therefore, it is an independent witness to the tradition of Jesus' teachings. Critics rightly note that this question is not settled among scholars in general. However, most critics agree with the Seminar that Thomas contains sayings that are early and independent. This is very important, because it means that both the Seminar and nearly all its critics agree that Thomas cannot be left out of historical Jesus research.

Birger Pearson's analysis of the Seminar's use of Thomas is puzzling. He charges that the Seminar's assumptions about Thomas are "quite naive," but then points out that of all the sayings unique to Thomas, the Seminar found only two that it could plausibly trace to Jesus. Pearson agrees with these results and so, presumably, does not consider them naive. This is puzzling because one expects naive assumptions to produce naive results.

The clear implication, then, is that the Seminar's methods must have corrected for the alleged naiveté of its assumptions. This is high praise indeed, though I doubt very much that Pearson intended it.

An assumption about Thomas that I brought with me to the Seminar was naive: the assumption that Thomas would shed new light on the historical Jesus. This assumption proved to be unfounded. Of the sayings unique to Thomas, the Seminar voted none red and only two pink.

Judging from the Seminar's results, Thomas tells us almost nothing about Jesus that we didn't already know from the other gospels. Nevertheless, the Seminar's findings on Thomas show that this gospel makes a valuable contribution to our understanding of Jesus.

This aspect of the Seminar's work has not been noted by critics and so I want to draw attention to it here. If the Seminar is right in its assessment that Thomas is an independent source, then Thomas provides multiple independent attestation for a number of otherwise singly-attested canonical sayings. By my count, there are 32 such items. This means that the Jesus Seminar's use of Thomas has the result of increasing our confidence in the historical reliability of a good deal of canonical material. This needs to be appreciated because a few critics—like Johnson—presume that the Seminar's attention to Thomas is intended to challenge the authority of the canon. The reality is precisely the opposite.

4R One detail noted by most critics is the reference in *The Five Gospels* to an early "first edition" of Thomas. They object that there is no evidence for such a document.

Miller This objection is exactly right. The Seminar concludes that some sayings in Thomas are as early as their parallels in Mark and Q, and that a few may be even earlier. Thus the earliest layer of tradition in Thomas is as early as the earliest layer of the synoptic tradition. But the first time I saw or heard a reference to an early first edition of Thomas was in the Seminar's own publications.

To set the record straight as best I can, very few members of the Seminar subscribe to this theory and I consider it unfortunate that this new and controversial theory is put forth as if it were an established position. However, the substance of the claim that there was an early first edition is that Thomas contains material as early as the synoptics, something on which the Seminar and its critics essentially agree.

4R For the general public the most controversial aspect of the Jesus Seminar is that it does not accept the literal historicity of each verse in the gospels. But it appears that the most controversial item for scholars is that the Jesus of the Jesus Seminar is non-apocalyptic. [The Jesus Seminar's conclusion that Jesus was a non-apocalyptic teacher, that he did not expect the imminent end of the world, contradicts the commonly held view proposed by Albert Schweitzer in his 1906 book, *The Quest of the Historical Jesus*—ed.] Of all the Seminar's findings, why is this the one that its critics attack most vigorously?

Miller Critics charge that the non-apocalyptic Jesus was an a priori assumption for the Seminar and that we judged sayings to be inauthentic simply because they are apocalyptic. For example, Howard Kee refers to the Seminar's "manipulation of evidence in order to rid Jesus of an apocalyptic outlook," a procedure he calls "prejudgment masquerading as scholarship." Richard Hays asserts, the "Jesus Seminar employs its conviction that Jesus was a non-eschatological thinker as a stringent criterion for sorting the authenticity of the sayings material," and "an a priori construal of Jesus and his message governs the critical judgment made about individual sayings." Luke Johnson charges that Jesus' eschatology is "simply dismissed without significant argument."

From my perspective as a participant in the Seminar, I have to say that this is a major misunderstanding of what really went on in the Seminar.

I believe this misunderstanding results from two factors. The first is that, although *The Five Gospels* never actually says that apocalyptic sayings were assumed to be inauthentic, it does in some places give this impression, which is, to my mind, unfortunate because it is misleading. The second factor is the unwillingness of most critics of the Seminar to grant that any of its members has even half a brain or an ounce of integrity.

Since there is a good deal of misunderstanding about how the Seminar arrived at its conclusion, it may help if I relate my own experience. I joined the Seminar when my Ph.D. was barely one year old. I had not specialized in historical Jesus studies and had not thought very deeply about whether Jesus was an apocalyptic prophet. I assumed that he was because I had absorbed the common wisdom of New Testament scholarship.

In preparing for Seminar meetings over several years, I worked through all the apocalyptic sayings one by one. Though I was predisposed to consider this kind of material authentic, I was persuaded time and again by both the position papers and the debates to vote gray or black. Some learned and respected members argued in favor of the apocalyptic Jesus but the votes consistently went against them. Unfortunately, but understandably, most of the members who championed the apocalyptic Jesus eventually left the Seminar.

Some members had studied the issue extensively and had moved away from the apocalyptic portrait of Jesus before the Seminar had been formed. However, my impression is that most of us were like me: without strong positions either way and open to being persuaded by the evidence in the texts and the arguments of other scholars.

I am not implying that everyone who studies the material the way I did will reach the same conclusions. I am only saying that this is how it happened for me. I have no writings on this topic to defend and no scholarly reputation to uphold. This, plus my undistinguished academic position, testifies that I have no professional stake in this matter. There is a certain freedom in being marginal.

4R Birger Pearson writes that a non-apocalyptic Jesus "strains credulity to its breaking point." He makes the intriguing claim that even the sayings that the Seminar colored red and pink are shot through with apocalyptic eschatology.

Miller Pearson concludes that Seminar members were simply too stupid to notice this! Another conclusion at least as plausible as Pearson's is that, despite the Seminar's alleged ideologically driven effort to root out apocalyptic from the historical Jesus, its criteria and methods were so sound that they led the Seminar to results contrary to its ideology.

However, a far more realistic possibility is that these red and pink sayings need not be read apocalyptically. A number of these sayings acquire their apocalyptic coloring from their literary contexts, or from interpretive comments that are very probably secondary, or from the apocalyptic framework within which scholars place them. However, if considered on their own terms apart from their literary contexts, secondary interpretations, and exegetical frameworks, their apocalyptic character is far from obvious and, in many cases, just not there.

I believe this whole question is an open one. The presence and extent of apocalyptic in Jesus' sayings is an issue over which scholars can have an honest discussion, even a fair fight. For now I only want to point out the arbitrariness of the assumption that if a saying can be read apocalyptically, it must be read that way.

Nested with this assumption is another one that is seldom challenged: the assumption that the Palestine of Jesus' time was rife with apocalypticism. The premier evidence for this is, of course, the Dead Sea scrolls. However, the question relevant to the historical Jesus is whether there was pervasive apocalypticism in Galilee in the twenties of the first century CE and for this the scrolls are not very useful.

The current consensus on the Dead Sea scrolls is that they represent the views of a small, disaffected, and physically isolated sect. What about the Galilean day laborers, fishermen, shopkeepers, and marketplace scribes to whom Jesus spoke? What evidence do we have that allows us to reliably gauge their outlook? By the way, this would make an excellent topic for a dissertation. Are we so sure that we know enough about this to take for granted that Jesus' environment was all that apocalyptic?

4R Critics say that the non-apocalyptic Jesus of the Jesus Seminar would not have gotten crucified. If the historical Jesus was not an apocalyptic teacher, why was he killed?

Miller The assumption here is that the apocalyptic message—which may or may not include explicit or implicit messianic claims—is both the necessary and sufficient cause for Jesus' execution. But this assumption does not hold up under scrutiny. An apocalyptic message by itself does not get you killed. If it did, the entire Qumran community would have been snuffed out in a mass execution.

John the Baptist, even with his high public profile, was not executed for his apocalyptic message, but for his personal attacks on Herod. An apocalyptic message has to be combined with something else for its messenger to become a political threat. But this is as true for a non-apocalyptic message.

Wouldn't anyone who disrupted the temple on the scale that Jesus is reported to have done be perceived as a dangerous troublemaker, regardless of his message, or even if he had no particular message at all? One can argue that disrupting the temple is a symbolic act with an apocalyptic meaning, but this is not its only plausible interpretation.

But there is an assumption more fundamental than any of this, an assumption that exists virtually unchallenged in all historical Jesus research, within the Seminar and outside of it. The assumption is that there must have been a connection between Jesus' death and his teaching, that he was killed because of what he stood for. While this is obviously a reasonable assumption, it is not a necessary one.

Several prior assumptions are required to support it, for example: that the Romans crucified people only after they had properly determined their guilt and established that crucifixion was the proper punishment; that Jesus' teaching and activities were known by the Jewish authorities in Jerusalem prior to his arrival there; that these Jewish authorities, unlike his disciples, truly understood his teaching and its implications.

Without all of these assumptions, and others besides, we cannot confidently stipulate that Jesus must have been killed because of his message. It becomes plausible to imagine that his death was a routine act of state brutality by a military dictatorship, whose motive for the institution of crucifixion was not so much to punish the guilty as to terrorize the population. Crucifixion, after all, is not just a form of execution; it is a public spectacle, a theater of cruelty that burns into everyone's mind the absolute power of the state and their own vulnerability to it.

I am not asserting that there was no connection between Jesus' message and his death, only that this is an assumption that rests on several other assumptions, all of which may be true, but none of which is self-evident.

If the hesitation to grant any of those prior assumptions is in any way reasonable, then we need not assume that Jesus was necessarily executed because of what he taught. We certainly do not need to assume that Jesus would not have been killed unless he had had an apocalyptic message.

4R Probably the most bitter criticism of the Seminar is that its Jesus is not Jewish. Richard Hays suggests that the Seminar's portrait of Jesus is a fiction achieved by the "surgical removal of Jesus from his Jewish context," and that the creation of a non-Jewish Jesus is a "particularly pernicious side effect of the Jesus Seminar's methodology." What exactly does it mean that the Jesus of the Jesus Seminar is not Jewish?

Miller Birger Pearson takes Hays' surgical imagery even further! He says that the Jesus Seminar has "performed a forcible epispasm on the historical Jesus, a surgical procedure removing the marks of his circumcision." Believe it or not, that sentence was actually written by a respected scholar and published in a journal of the highest caliber.

The Jesus of the Jesus Seminar is the implied author/speaker of the parables and aphorisms that the Seminar colored red

and pink. Therefore, to claim that this Jesus is not Jewish can
only mean that the implied speaker of the Good Samaritan
and the Prodigal Son, the one who invoked God as "abba"
and pronounced blessings on the poor, and so on—that whoever said these things was not Jewish. I doubt that critics really
intend this judgment, but if they do not, then the accusation
that the Seminar's Jesus is not Jewish lacks specific content and
so should be regarded as vacuous rhetoric.

Stepping back from the rhetorical heat of this accusation,
we can tease out an assumption on which it is founded. This
assumption is that we know enough about Galilean Judaism in
the first third of the first century to be able to recognize what
could and could not have been part of it. Does anyone really
want to own that assumption? If not, the criticism evaporates
because there are no secure grounds on which it could be
either substantiated or rebutted.

I conclude that the Jewishness of Jesus is not a real issue of
honest academic debate. The accusation that the Jesus Seminar
strips Jesus of his Judaism is a powerful attention-getter, but
it is an accusation without specific content. Everyone in the
historical Jesus debate agrees that Jesus was Jewish. The real
question is what kind of Jew he was.

Whether or not the historical Jesus was Jewish is a phony
question, but it carries an assumption that is well worth explor-
ing. This is the assumption that identity is constituted by mark-
ers of distinctiveness. Only on this assumption could one reason
that if a given reconstruction of the historical Jesus does not
make topics like covenant, law, messiah, and apocalyptic central
to Jesus' teaching then that Jesus is not Jewish. This is rather like
saying that I must not be Catholic because I don't put the Mass
or the Pope at the center of my religious language.

4R This raises the question of the criterion of dissimilarity,
also a favorite target of critics.

Miller Yes. In fact, the Seminar ran aground on this issue
repeatedly and debated it vigorously on numerous occasions.
Eventually most of us seem to have settled on a soft version of
dissimilarity that Robert Funk calls "distinctiveness."

If Jesus' speech was not distinctive in his own Jewish context, then why did people bother to remember it and pass it on? If it is not distinctive vis-a-vis later Christian speech, then, by definition, we cannot distinguish the voice of Jesus from the voice of the church, and therefore the search for the historical Jesus is futile. So if you accept the viability of historical Jesus research, you cannot avoid the criterion of distinctiveness.

Most everyone agrees that the criterion is especially helpful in principle, but applying it can prove troublesome in concrete cases. The criterion produces minimalist results; it cannot do otherwise. Jesus obviously said and did more than what is historically verifiable with this criterion.

4R How then do you move beyond the minimalist results to include material that is not distinctive?

Miller The Seminar is divided on this question. For us it comes down to how we regard the material we've colored gray. The Seminar has more than one meaning for the gray vote. One is "maybe historical, maybe not;" another is "Jesus didn't say this, but it is based on his ideas." Thus you can regard a gray vote as either a negative or a positive vote. If you consult the voting results, you can see that for many gray items there was a considerable percentage of red and pink votes.

There is a lot of gray material. Many members of the Seminar, myself included, treat the gray material as a fund from which to expand the database for the historical Jesus beyond the red and pink minimum. The only items excluded in principle from the database are those colored black. One of the definitions of the gray vote is: "I would not include this item in the database, but I might make use of some of the content in determining who Jesus was." So, gray items can be considered on a case-by-case basis. This means that the working database for many of us is substantially larger than the 18% of the sayings that are red and pink.

4R This figure of 18% has gotten a lot of attention. The Seminar's critics all use it to show how skeptical the Seminar is. How should the public understand it?

Miller Consider what this 18% is 18% of. The 90 red and pink sayings are 18% of all the sayings attributed to Jesus in all Christian texts from the first three centuries, including gospels the Seminar unanimously voted black in their entirety, such as the Dialogue of the Savior, the Secret Book of James, the Gospel of Mary, and the Infancy Gospel of Thomas. Regarding the Gospel of John, I believe it is fair to say that most Jesus scholars outside the Seminar would agree with us that few, if any, sayings in it are demonstrably authentic.

So, if we set the range of the database to be the sayings in Matthew, Mark, Luke, and Thomas, and if we realize that a good deal of the gray material can be included, the percentage of sayings in the database is significantly larger than 18%. My conservative guess is that it is probably around 50% for most of us and even higher for some.

4R So, in your judgment, what really is at stake in the debate between the Seminar and its critics?

Miller A lot is at stake, but three things strike me as most important. The first is the civility of scholarly discourse. By that I mean the willingness of scholars to debate the issues without resorting to *ad hominem* arguments or personal attacks on opponents, without misrepresenting or distorting others' positions, and without indulging in ridicule or insinuation.

The second crucial thing I think is at stake is the integrity to own up to one's assumptions. In this case that means acknowledging that the Seminar's general assumptions about the gospels and its basic methods of historical inquiry are shared by virtually all scholars who are committed to the historical-critical study of the Bible.

The third vital issue at stake is the duty of biblical scholars to educate the public. In this case that means the courage and willingness to come clean, to say to the public what we have long said to one another, to communicate clearly and honestly the results of critical scholarship on the historical Jesus.

4R Any closing comments?

Miller Yes. I would like to take a moment to reflect on the rancorous tone of some of the Seminar's critics. The pettiness and nastiness of some of the criticisms of the Seminar shows that the Seminar's work has hit a nerve. The issues at stake are more than academic, and it is natural that some will have strong feelings about them.

That is no excuse, however, for debasing the discussion with personal attacks. Even if a few readers relish the spectacle of scholars slinging mud at one another, incivility in scholarly discourse distracts attention and energy from the real task, that of increasing our understanding.

I trust that everyone in the historical Jesus debate, regardless of his or her religious beliefs, sincerely desires to increase our understanding of Jesus and does so out of respect for him and what he has left us. Jesus' teaching is unambiguous about how we should relate to opponents. Honest disagreement is not to be avoided, for it can lead to greater understanding. What we disagree about is indeed important, but so is how we disagree. We should all conduct this debate about Jesus in a manner that honors his teaching and his memory.

Works Consulted

Boring, M. Eugene. "Criteria of Authenticity: The Lucan Beatitudes as a Test Case." *Forum* 1 (1985): 3–38.

_____, *Sayings of the Risen Jesus.* Society for New Testament Studies Monograph Series 46. Cambridge: Cambridge University Press, 1982.

Borg, Marcus J. "A Temperate Case for a Non-Eschatological Jesus." *Forum* 2 (September 1986): 81–102.

_____, "Jesus Was Not an Apocalyptic Prophet." In *The Apocalyptic Jesus: A Debate,* edited by Robert Miller. Santa Rosa: Polebridge Press, 2001.

Bornkamm, Gunther. *Jesus of Nazareth.* Translated by Irene and Fraser McLuskey with James M. Robinson. New York.: Harper and Row, 1960 (first German edition 1956).

Bultmann, Rudolf. *History of the Synoptic Tradition.* Rev ed. Translated by John Marsh. New York: Harper and Row, 1963 (German edition 1921).

Crossan, John Dominic. *In Fragments: The Aphorisms of Jesus.* San Francisco: Harper & Row, 1983. Reprint, Santa Rosa, CA: Polebridge Press.

_____, *In Parables: The Challenge of the Historical Jesus.* New York, Harper and Row, 1973. Reprint, Santa Rosa, CA: Polebridge Press.

_____, *Four Other Gospels: Shadows on the Contours of Canon.* Minneapolis: Winston Press, 1985.

Dibelius, Martin. *From Tradition to Gospel.* Translated by Bertram Lee Woolf. New York: Scribner, 1965 (first German edition 1919).

Dodd, C. H. *The Parables of the Kingdom.* New York: Scribner, 1961 (first published in 1936).

Friedman, Edwin H. *Generation to Generation: Family Process in Church and Synagogue.* New York: Guilford Press, 1985.

Funk, Robert W. *Honest to Jesus: Jesus for a New Millennium*. San
    Francisco: HarperSanFrancisco, 1996.

_____, "The Issue of Jesus." See chapter 1 in this volume.

_____, *Language, Hermeneutic, and Word of God: The Problem of
    Language in the New Testament and Contemporary Theology*. New
    York: Harper & Row, 1966. See Robert W. Funk, *Funk on
    Parables*. Santa Rosa: Polebridge Press, 2006.

Funk, Robert W., Roy W. Hoover and the Jesus Seminar. *The Five
    Gospels: The Search for the Authentic Words of Jesus*. New York:
    Macmillan Publishing Company, 1993.

Funk, Robert W. and the Jesus Seminar. *The Acts of Jesus: Search for the
    Authentic Deeds of Jesus*. San Francisco: HarperSanFrancisco, 1998.

Funk, Robert W., Bernard Brandon Scott and James R. Butts. *The
    Parables of Jesus: Red Letter Edition*. Santa Rosa, CA: Polebridge
    Press, 1988.

Harvey, Van A. *The Historian and the Believer. The Morality of Historical
    Knowledge and Christian Belief*. New York: Macmillan, 1966.

Hays, Richard. "The Corrected Jesus." *First Things* 43 (May 1994):
    43-48.

Jeremias, Joachim. *The Parables of Jesus*. Translated by S. H. Hooke.
    New York: Charles Scribner's Sons, 1963 (based on the sixth
    German edition of 1962).

Johnson, Luke. "The Jesus Seminar's Misguided Quest for the
    Historical Jesus." *The Christian Century* (January 3-10, 1996),
    16-22.

_____, *The Real Jesus*. San Francisco: HarperSanFrancisco, 1995.

Johnson, Vernon E. *I'll Quit Tomorrow*. San Francisco: Harper & Row,
    1980.

Käsemann, Ernst. "The Problem of the Historical Jesus." In *Essays on
    New Testament Themes*. Translated by W. J. Montague. Studies in
    Biblical Theology. London: SCM Press, 1964.

Kee, Howard. "A Century of Quests for the Culturally Compatible
    Jesus." *Theology Today* 52 (April 1995): 17-28.

Kelber, Werner H. *The Oral and the Written Gospel: The Hermeneutics
    of Speaking and Writing in the Synoptic Tradition, Mark, Paul, and
    Q*. Philadelphia: Fortress Press, 1983. Reprint, Bloomington, IN:
    Indiana University Press.

Kermode, Frank. *The Sense of an Ending: Studies in the Theory of
    Fiction*. Oxford: Oxford University Press, 1967.

Kerr, Michael E. and Murray Bowen. *Family Evaluation.* New York: W. W. Norton & Company, 1988.

King, Karen L. "Kingdom in the Gospel of Thomas." *Forum* 1,1 (1985): 23–29.

Kloppenborg, John S. *The Formation of Q: Trajectories in Ancient Wisdom Collections.* Studies in Antiquity & Christianity. Philadelphia: Fortress Press, 1987.

Koester, Helmut. *Ancient Christian Gospels: Their History and Development.* Philadelphia: Trinity Press International, 1990.

Mack, Burton. "The Kingdom Sayings in Mark." *Forum* 3,1 (1987): 3–47.

Metzger, Bruce. *The Canon of the New Testament.* Oxford: Oxford University Press, 1987.

Miller, Robert J., ed. *The Complete Gospels.* Santa Rosa, CA: Polebridge Press, 1994.

_____, *The Jesus Seminar and Its Critics.* Santa Rosa, CA: Polebridge Press, 1999.

Pearson, Birger. "The Gospel According to the Jesus Seminar." *Religion* 25 (December 1995): 317-38.

Pelikan, Jaroslav. *The Vindication of Tradition.* New Haven and London: Yale University Press, 1984. The quotations about tradition and traditionalism appear on pages 65, 70 and 73.

Perrin, Norman. *The Kingdom of God in the Teaching of Jesus.* New Testament Library. Philadelphia: Westminster Press, 1963.

_____, *Rediscovering the Teaching of Jesus.* New York: Harper and Row, 1967.

Powell, Mark Allan. *Jesus as a Figure in History: How Modern Historians View the Man from Galilee.* Louisville: Westminster John Knox Press, 1998.

Robinson, James M. *A New Quest of the Historical Jesus.* Studies in Biblical Theology. London: SCM Press, 1959.

Schweitzer, Albert. *The Quest of the Historical Jesus: A Critical Study of Its Progress from Reimarus to Wrede.* Translated by W. Montgomery. New York: Macmillan, 1910. Reprinted 1968 (first German edition 1906).

Scott, Bernard Brandon. "Essaying the Rock: The Authenticity of the Jesus Parable Tradition." *Forum* 2 (1986): 3–35.

_____, *Hear Then the Parable.* Minneapolis: Fortress Press, 1989.

_____, *Jesus, Symbol-Maker for the Kingdom*. Philadelphia: Fortress, 1981.

Tannehill, Robert C. *The Sword of His Mouth*. Philadelphia: Fortress Press, 1975.

Via, Dan O. *The Parables: Their Literary and Existential Dimension*. Philadelphia: Fortress Press, 1967.

Wilder, Amos Niven. *The Language of the Gospel: Early Christian Rhetoric*. New York: Harper and Row, 1964.

Wilkins, Michael J. and J. P. Moreland, eds. *Jesus under Fire*. Grand Rapids: Zondervan, 1995.

Witherington III, Ben. *The Jesus Quest*. Downers Grove: Intervarsity Press, 1995.

Questions
for Discussion

Chapter 1
Robert W. Funk, *The Issue of Jesus*

1. Why will this project of discovering what Jesus actually said strike some as dangerous or even blasphemous? Why does this continue to be so?
2. Why is it important to really know what Jesus said and did?
3. Why does Funk think scholarship needs to be cumulative, reciprocal and public?
4. Funk calls for a new fiction about Jesus. What do you think he means by "fiction" and what might that new fiction be?

Chapter 2
Roy W. Hoover, *The Work of the Jesus Seminar*

1. What kind of new evidence was available to scholars at the beginning of the Jesus Seminar that had not been available previously?
2. Why had scholarship in the past not gone public, and what is the significance of making scholarship public?
3. How does voting affect the decisions of the Seminar? Does it create confidence in the Seminar's work or is it catering to democracy?
4. If a camel is a horse designed by a committee, is the collaborative work of the Seminar only a committee effort or does collaboration produce a better way of sorting the evidence.
5. What criteria do you think are most important in deciding what comes from Jesus?

6. If something does not come from Jesus, what theological authority does it have? Likewise, if something does come from Jesus, what theological significance does it have?

Chapter 3

Marcus J. Borg, *The Making of* The Five Gospels

1. What makes the Jesus Seminar "unprecedented"?
2. What is the difference between, "Red means Jesus said it" and "Red means a very strong scholarly consensus that Jesus said it"?
3. Why is the discovery of the Gospel of Thomas important for the study of the historical Jesus?
4. The most controversial finding of the Jesus Seminar is that Jesus did not predict the end of the world or his own second coming. Rather the Kingdom of God is present. What is the basis for this statement?
5. Borg gives three reasons for rejecting the Lord's Prayer as coming directly from Jesus. How do you evaluate this decision?

Chapter 4

Perry V. Kea, *The Road to the Jesus Seminar*

1. Miracles (divine intervention) are a normal expectation for a pre-Enlightenment mentality, but impossible for the post-Enlightenment mentality. Why?
2. The earliest stage of the quest (pre-WWI) sought the earliest written source for a life of Jesus. But Form Critics showed that the earliest tradition was oral. How does this affect the effort to write a life of Jesus?
3. How something is expressed is an important contributor to its meaning, that is, you cannot separate the "message" from its container. How does this change the view of Jesus' parables and aphorisms?
4. If the future/apocalyptic Son of Man sayings are the product of the early church, how does this affect the view of Jesus as a prophet?
5. When the Jesus Seminar claims a historical core for the exorcisms, what is it claiming?

Chapter 5
Bernard Brandon Scott, *How Did We Get Here?*

1. How does the criterion of dissimilarity determine what comes from Jesus? What in your judgment is its strength(s) and weakness(es)?
2. Why was the layering of Q into, first, wisdom and, then, apocalyptic levels important for understanding the historical Jesus?
3. Why is the Gospel of Thomas important in our reconstruction of the historical Jesus?
4. Why are Luke 17:20 21 and Gospel of Thomas 113 important in determining whether Jesus' view of the Kingdom is apocalyptic or wisdom? What is the significance of this decision?
5. If you were constructing a collection of Gospels, what would you include, in what order and why?

Chapter 6
Ruth Schweitzer-Mordecai, *The Jesus Intervention*

1. What do you think are the chief "family secrets" of the church?
2. Is scholarship about Jesus, done in the public eye, healthy and proper or is it part of the TV age seeking after fifteen minutes of fame?
3. What is the crisis provoked by the quest for the historical Jesus? Where do you see it leading you? The church?
4. Does the model of family systems help illuminate the church's crisis?

Chapter 7
Roy W. Hoover, *Answering the Critics*

1. For Brock the authentic words of Jesus are the confessions of the later Christians. Why does he take this position? What then is Jesus' function?
2. The view of the task of history has shifted. Traditionally, the task of history was to support the reliability of the gospels. Then it shifted to evaluate the reliability of the gospels. What caused this shift?

3. What is the task of the historian? What is the task of the theologian? What in your judgment is the relation between these two?

Chapter 8

Robert J. Miller, *The Jesus Seminar and Its Critics*

1. What are the primary criticisms of the Jesus Seminar? Does Miller answer them adequately?
2. Is there a common thread to these criticisms?
3. What is your critique of the findings of the Jesus Seminar?
4. What is the value of the Jesus Seminar?

Notes

Notes